So you've been asked to plan the next big (or small) church event. Such a request strikes fear in the heart and a barrage of questions flood the mind. The good news is *God Is in the Details* is your answer. Lynne Shivers, an experienced _____ t planner and seasoned minister, has penned this groundbreaking _____ tool for individuals who have been tasked with planning a _____ sents a biblical-base foundation for planning events that _____ step-by-step instructions for event planning are use_____ _____ churches or secular arenas. If you have a passion for excelle_____ _____ *Details* is for you.

_____ DEBBY MITCHELL, FOUNDER
All Things Artistic Ministries, Inc. Christian Writers

Prior to my retirement from *Joy of Jesus Ministries* in Detroit, I planned and successfully implemented many events. However, I have learned one thing for sure after editing Lynne Shivers' comprehensive book, *God Is in the Details;* there is always more that we can learn. It is a wonderful resource tool for all event planners. Oh, how much I wish that I would have had this awesome book "back in the day." It has been a pleasure to serve as Lynne Shivers' editor. Do yourself a favor and get a copy before you plan your next event.

—MINISTER MARY D. EDWARDS
Leaves of Gold Consulting, LLC

For the past seven years I have prayed, cried, worried, put notes on paper and then lost the paper trying to prepare for a successful conference. Attending another conference, as the Lord would have it, I met Evangelist Lynne Shivers and in conversing I mentioned to her concerning my conference. As we talked she informed me that she was an event planner and that the Lord had instructed her to help me take the conference to the next level. As we journeyed through the planning time line and her blueprint of P.E.A.C.E.; her expertise, wisdom and knowledge, eliminated all doubts, fears, and removed the struggles. Needless to say, it was the best and most successful conference since its inception. Lynne's knowledge of event planning is God sent to the religious community.

—DR. EULA PAYNE-WILLIAMS
President/CEO
Bruised But Not Broken Conference

God

Is in the

Details

PEACEful Event Planning for
Churches and Religious Groups

LYNNE E. SHIVERS

WESTBOW°
PRESS
A DIVISION OF THOMAS NELSON
& ZONDERVAN

Unless otherwise indicated, scripture are taken from the King James Version of the Bible.

Scripture quotations marked (NIV) are taken from the Holy Bible, New International Version®,
NIV®. Copyright © 1973, 1978, 1984, 2011 by Biblica, Inc.™ Used by permission of Zondervan.
All rights reserved worldwide. www.zondervan.com The "NIV" and "New International Version"
are trademarks registered in the United States Patent and Trademark Office by Biblica, Inc.™

WestBow Press books may be ordered through booksellers or by contacting:

WestBow Press
A Division of Thomas Nelson & Zondervan
1663 Liberty Drive
Bloomington, IN 47403
www.westbowpress.com
1 (866) 928-1240

Because of the dynamic nature of the Internet, any web addresses or links contained
in this book may have changed since publication and may no longer be valid. The views
expressed in this work are solely those of the author and do not necessarily reflect the
views of the publisher, and the publisher hereby disclaims any responsibility for them.

Any people depicted in stock imagery provided by Thinkstock are models,
and such images are being used for illustrative purposes only.
Certain stock imagery © Thinkstock.

ISBN: 978-1-4908-2462-8 (sc)
ISBN: 978-1-4908-2461-1 (e)

Library of Congress Control Number: 2014901920

Printed in the United States of America.

WestBow Press rev. date: 04/21/2014

CONTENTS

Chapter 15

Part 5

Chapter 16

Part 6

Chapter 17

Part 7

Chapter 18

Tools for Success

PEACEFUL
Quiet; undisturbed; not in a state of war or commotion.[1]

"Thou wilt keep him in perfect peace, whose mind is
stayed on thee: because he trusteth in thee."
—Isaiah 26:3

---

[1] *King James Bible Page, www. http://av1611.com/kjbp/kjv-dictionary/peace.html*

PREFACE

Thank You, Lord. I give first thanks to God, my Lord and Savior Jesus Christ, for allowing me to finally finish this book. It has taken years to complete. It seemed to be an eternal work in progress and a burning desire that I could not shake as I taught workshops and minicourses on event planning at colleges. Somehow, someway I had to write a book for churches and religious groups—His people. God is the master event planner. As He is excellent in all of His ways, we see His magnificent work every day. It's been ten years since I wrote these first pages for Him, which now are given to you.

I hope you will find *God Is in the Details* helpful as you plan your Christian-focused event. It has truly been written from my heart. I have shared not only my successes, but also my mistakes and mishaps, with hopes that you will learn from my experiences and not repeat the same. My prayer is that you will have *peace*, that all of your events will be blessed, that God will get all the glory, and His children will be edified, refreshed, and restored because of your efforts.

May God's peace be with you,

Lynne E. Shivers

ACKNOWLEDGMENTS

As I finish my first book, I realize now how many people have helped me through the years to get to this point. I cannot remember everyone, but to each and every one of you, I say thank you. Whether it was a timely word or a disappointed stare when I told you the book was not done, thank you.

To my loving husband, Jonathan. Your love and undying support have been a strength that has helped me through my most difficult times. Thank you, sweetie.

To Melanie, my daughter. You are so very special to me. May God continue to bless you in ways that exceed whatever you could ask for or think of. This book being completed is a testimony of what God can do if we believe in Him.

Dr. Debby Mitchell, you provided insight, encouragement, and a swift kick when I needed it the most. You kept me to my promise to get it done. It's a little later than I had planned, but thank you!

To my long-time friend, LaTanya Orr of Selah Branding & Design LLC, thank you for the design of my book cover.

To my pastor, Bishop Gary Harper, thank you for always saying, "Carry on, soldier." I am sure you did not realize that those inspiring words were helping me to keep going until I finished this book.

INTRODUCTION

"I'm overwhelmed and have no help. My event is next week and I'm scared." I'll never forget those words spoken by a young woman attending my event planning class. The quiver in her voice and frustration on her face caused my heart to go out to her. Nearly in tears she said, "I don't have any help and there are two hundred people attending my event." She did not know where to start. Time had slipped away. Seven days out and only a few minor things had been completed. Everything seemed to have the same priority. Everything seemed equally important. Everything seemed too much. A spirit of fear had gripped her. She felt paralyzed with no help in sight. I spent the next few minutes giving her suggestions to work on immediately. She was able to identify tasks and who should complete them. She left the workshop feeling more in control. It was not unmanageable. She just needed to know what to do.

If you are feeling bombarded with all the myriad of details in planning an event, you are not alone. We must remember that our battle is not flesh and blood. God gives us the answers. *God Is in the Details* gives Christian event planners a reference guide to quickly get information on planning their *Spirit-led* event. While the how-tos and important steps will be outlined, more importantly, readers will understand the critical differences that take an event from mediocre to memorable.

This book is for those of you who have felt apprehensive about accepting the role of event coordinator. In fact, you still remember that day when the pastor or official asked for a volunteer to chair the event and you raised your hand. There you were, looking at your raised hand and giving a stupefied nod. Without totally understanding all the details, without knowing what should be done first, you stepped out on faith to lead the planning of the next church retreat, Family and Friends Day, prayer breakfast, or spiritual conference.

Maybe you have planned events in the past, but you are looking for more direction on planning a God-directed event. You understand the gravity of this responsibility. The event should not only satisfy the attendees, but most importantly, glorify Christ.

This book is for you! It will help you understand the skills that reduce the stress associated with planning events. You have looked down the road that lies ahead, and it seems daunting. You may even think that because you are not trained in the area of event planning or do not have a grasp of the industry lingo, you are not up for the job. Self-doubt and worry step in—two of the Devil's devices to sabotage God's purpose for the event. The ever-looming event may have already begun to consume you in ways you never thought of. You are being pulled on every side and expected to have answers to so many questions. The event may be weeks or months away, and you have already spent many worrying hours wondering and hoping that you are on the right track.

The Devil bombards us with the what-ifs. "What if no one shows up?" "What if it's a disaster?" "What if I fail?" Stop kicking yourself for not responding in the beginning with that liberating two-letter word no! You can do this! God has appointed you for such a time as this. Believe in your heart that you can have a great event, and in the process, God will use you in ways you never imagined.

God Is in the Details covers the essential steps to planning an event, as well as working with others in the church—from the pastor to members on the committee to those in the congregation. Chapter 8 is devoted to the chairperson's role and relationship to the committee. Too often the tensions of these relationships can cause us to have inappropriate attitudes, sow discord, and create disunity. "Let us do everything decently and in order" (1 Cor. 14:40). You will learn how to have control over the planning, and not the planning over you. The Bible tells us to be wise to Satan's tactics. When we realize that we are fighting an invisible enemy who will try to thwart the success of the event, we will think about the planning much differently. The Enemy's goal is to disrupt the planning process and cause conflict and infighting, so that even if the event does occur, the seed of discord has been planted.

Contained also are helpful tips throughout the book, as well as encouraging Scriptures and prayers. The ultimate and final reward from God is to hear, "Well done, my good and faithful servant." We must keep in mind that everything we do or say is a reflection of our relationship with Him. As we strive to please Him, we will reap an eternal reward.

God Is in the Details will introduce you to the life cycle of event planning, which I have called P.E.A.C.E.: **P**ray and Project-planning time line, **E**xecute, **A**djust,

Communicate and control, and **E**valuate. Using this process, we will explore the specific charge of each phase and demonstrate how the process can produce a well-planned and organized event.

When we keep God as the master planner, seeking His direction throughout the process, we will indeed have a P.E.A.C.E.*ful* event.

Lynne Shivers

AUTHOR'S NOTE

The information I have provided in this book is a compilation of more than thirty years' experience in the event-planning field. As with any professional desiring to stay on top of current trends and information, I have attended event-management conferences and event-planning and project-planning workshops, read numerous books, and received advice from many event managers. As I have incorporated much of the information that is available on event planning, I created a system that worked for me as I approached planning an event. I believe what I have created is my own unique approach to planning an event that will be useful to anyone— whether you are planning a church event or not. If anything in this book looks familiar to other planning time lines, it is because there is a general approach to planning that is consistent across the field.

PART 1

THE IMPORTANCE OF CHRISTIAN AND RELIGIOUS EVENTS

"The steps of a good man are ordered by the Lord:
and he delighteth in his way."
—Psalm 37:23

Dear Lord,

I bless Your name. I give You all the praise, honor, and majesty. Thank You for showing me through the Holy Scriptures more about You as the master event planner. Your ways are past finding out, but yet we see a glimpse of who You are throughout all creation. Everything Your hand has touched is beautiful. Each day that You created the earth, sun, stars, and heavens—and even mankind—has been an event! I thank You for Your guidance and how Your spirit directs my every step. I thank You now for speaking to my heart and helping me to understand how important events are to You.

Lord, help me to glean from the Scriptures ideas for my events. Help me to look past the obvious and easy ways to plan, and develop creative and exciting ways that sustain your children's interest. Help me to remember that I am planning an event for You. Keep me from all evil and deliver me from temptation. Lord, I acknowledge that I need Your help in all things. Help me to pray always and not faint. Help me to use wisdom in my speech and keep love in my heart. Have Your way this day. Have Your way throughout each step of the process. Have Your way on the big day. I say now and I will say then,

Amen.

CHAPTER 1

BIBLICAL EVENTS

"In the beginning God ..."
—Genesis 1:1a

God, the First Event Planner

It has been declared that "God is past finding out." Called many names throughout the ages, such as Savior, provider, healer, and deliverer, He has an equally accurate and prominent name that enables us to see another dimension of our great God. It may not appear as obvious as the other names that He is more closely affiliated with, but it makes perfect sense when examined. The God of creation, the omnipotent One, is also a masterful event planner. From the time He spoke into being heaven, earth, stars, animals, fowls, sea creatures, and humans, He has orchestrated a creative symphony, with each piece stepping into its role and purpose as needed and as ordained by Him.

Fast-forward several thousand or million years, and we follow amazing actions of our God: the creation, rise, and fall of humanity; the destruction of humankind—except for eight souls; the rebuilding of humankind, the called few, a nation born; the enslaving of Israel; and the delivering of His people, and their disobedience and subsequent captivity. Then something remarkable happens in the way that God starts to deal with His people. Besides having His prophets speak His words to exact chastisement or encouragement, He uses another instrument, a physical activity beyond *words* to tie their relationship—*events*. The many festivals, feasts, and celebrations that He established are outlined in the Bible. We see the first formal events in the book of Leviticus, and then they continue throughout the rest of the books of the Bible.

Why events? I often wondered why God would use such a complicated vehicle for His people to manage. My goodness, if Israel could not even wait a few days for Moses to come down from Mount Sinai before making golden images to worship, how were they to follow God's instructions to the letter of how He should be worshiped in an event? I believe God knew their difficulty with this assignment, as He left nothing to chance. He gave explicit instructions to the children of Israel explaining exactly how the festivals and holy celebrations would be handled. Every task was intricately spelled out, and such specificity ensured there would be no confusion about His expectations for the final result.

A general definition of a *festival* is "a public celebration that conveys, through a kaleidoscope of activities, certain meanings to participants and spectators."[2] We learn that God's festivals had both *meaning* and *purpose*. God created humans to be in fellowship with Him, and that desire would extend throughout all eternity (Eph. 2:7): "That in the ages to come he might show the exceeding riches of his grace in his kindness toward us through Christ Jesus."

Events and festivals have been organized for thousands of years, although many of these events were not to honor God but to pacify fleshly lusts or worship of pagan gods. One memorable feast often retold is found in the book of Esther. In chapter 1 verses 3–6, King Xerxes sponsors a lavish feast for all the dignitaries who report to him. This particular feast lasted 140 days (v. 4). The feast culminates with another party for all the servants in the palace, which went on for another seven days! And what an exhibition of royalty the servants beheld. Verse 6 describes the drapery colors of white, green, and blue, and how they were tied with cords of fine purple linen with silver rings. The beds they lounged on were made of gold and silver, upon a "pavement of red, and blue and white, and black marble" (v. 6).

Queen Vashti also holds a feast for the women in the royal house. One theologian writes,

---

[2]   Joe Goldblatt and Kathleen S. Nelson, *The International Dictionary of Event Management (The Wiley Event Management Series)* (New York: John Wiley & Sons, Inc., 2001), p. 78.

The women did not have banquets in the same room with the men. This separation of the sexes is an ancient custom that was observed at this time in the court of Persia, although one commentator, speaking of the custom, says that Babylon and Persia must, however, be looked upon as exceptions, where the ladies were not excluded from the festivals of the men (Daniel 5:2), and if we may believe the testimony of ancient authors, at Babylon they were not noted for their modesty on such occasions.[3]

Adapting Ideas from the Bible

God established festivals and feasts to demonstrate a marked difference in people's activities and His expectations. The Bible tells us that God's thoughts are not our thoughts, and His ways are not our ways (Isa. 55:8). This marked difference has not changed over thousands of years. Even in these modern times, we have to be consciously careful to distinguish our events so as not to confuse their purposes. We see vast differences in God-ordained events:

- They were appointed or set *by* God and were sacred or holy assemblies that were held on very special days.
- The holidays included a time of worship, as well as a time of great joy and festivity.
- The holidays focused upon the salvation and redemption of humanity and the worship of God.
- The holidays painted the prophetic picture of salvation, the salvation that God was to bring to people through His Son, the Lord Jesus Christ.
- The holidays showed a believer how he was to walk day by day throughout life.[4]

---

[3] J. M. Freeman, *The New Manners Customs of the Bible* (North Brunswick, NJ: Bridge-Logos Publishers, 1998), *p. 294.*

[4] See R. D. Robinson, *Bible Study: The Seven Feasts of Israel Leviticus 23:1–44. http:www. brandonweb.com/sermons/sermonpages/leviticus2.htm, p. 294*

Another significant consideration about the events God established was the effort to achieve excellence when they were executed. The Bible shows that God did not have an event for just any purpose, nor were they orchestrated because there had not been one for a while, nor to showcase the church's repertoire in displaying an impressive array of seminars, conferences, or meetings. Rather, His primary focus was using the event to demonstrate His concern for the salvation of His people and His desire of their devoted worship to Him.

Events *in* the house of God should contain at least one of these three primary purposes: convey God's love for His people, edify believers, and save those who are lost. God is concerned about souls. And ultimately, we should be too.

It's His house. God has stated clearly, as recorded in 276 Scriptures in the Bible, that the church building is referred to as the "house of God." Since the event is in *His* house, it's important that we seek His direction on the planning so that the end result will have His approval. How do we do this? Proverbs 3:6 says, "In all thy ways acknowledge him and he shall direct thy paths."

An Event-Planning Element That Is Important to God

When we look at the design elements of God, we notice something interesting—how the Bible describes who God is and what He does. From Genesis to Revelation, the Bible shows that our God has done excellent things and that this is known in all the earth (Isa. 12:5). He created an excellent salvation, which exceeds all others, and by this relationship we are complete in Him and need no other god (Col. 2:10). He created an excellent righteousness that exceeds the righteousness of all others, one that is perfect, pure, spotless, and everlasting. He offered up an excellent sacrifice, a sacrifice that excels all that was offered up under the law. And He has obtained an excellent victory over all His and His people's enemies: sin, Satan, and the world![5]

In Genesis 1:31, when God saw everything that He had made, He concluded it was *very* good. One definition of *excellent* is "very good or extremely good."[6]

---

[5] B. B. Biblos, *Gill's Exposition of the Entire Bible*. Biblehub: *http:bible.cc/isaiah/12-5.htm*.

[6] *The Merriam-Webster Dictionary.www.merriam-webster.com/dictionary/excellent*.

Too often we can place a hardship on ourselves in trying to make something *perfect*, when all God may be asking is that it be excellent. *Perfect* means "being entirely without fault or defect."[7] In our fallen state, perfection is impossible. But excellence is reachable—with the help of God. God is the one who determines when something meets His satisfaction. The spirit of perfection will cause you to never be satisfied with any final product. You will keep kicking yourself over tiny details that no one will really see and that don't really matter. Yes, we should strive for excellence, but excellence does not mean that you must be perfect. It means that you use your talents, abilities, and skills in the best way possible by taking an objective and critical look at each thing to see if it can be done better.

Strive to make the event God's version of "very or extremely good." Do not stress yourself over those things that you cannot change. If certain aspects are nice to have but not critical, weigh the importance and decide that only if you have time will you implement those items. If not, leave it alone. It will be okay. Most of us know the Serenity Prayer composed by Reinhold Niebuhr, but not in its entirety. The full version reads,

> God, grant me the serenity to accept the things I cannot change; courage to change the things I can; and wisdom to know the difference.
>
> Living one day at a time; enjoying one moment at a time; accepting hardships as the pathway to peace; taking, as He did, this sinful world as it is, not as I would have it; trusting that He will make all things right if I surrender to His will; that I may be reasonably happy in this life and supremely happy with Him forever in the next. Amen.

How liberating to know that there are some things you cannot change! Leave those things to God. Bishop Clifton Jones, a pastor who has written many books, states it this way in a text message to followers: "Did you know worry is life's worst paralysis? It would definitely keep one from walking in faith."

Do the best you can and leave the rest to God. God can tell you what needs to be done. Remember, God is the only one who is perfect and excellent in all His ways.

---

[7] *Merriam-Webster Dictionary. www.merriam-webster.com/dictionary/perfect.*

CHAPTER 2

CHURCH IN REACH (THE "99")

"Those things, which ye have both learned, and received, and heard,
and seen in me, do: and the God of peace shall be with you."
—Philippians 4:9

Meeting the Needs of the Congregation

Since the time when the apostles began preaching and teaching the good gospel, churches began to form. From that time until today, there has been a robust development of churches in the body of Christ. An excerpt from the online *2011 Yearbook of American and Canadian Churches* reports that there are more than 227 national church bodies, with memberships of more than 145,838,339 people.[8] The *2010 U.S. Religion Census: Religion Congregations & Membership Study* estimates there are more than 344,000 Protestant and other Christian churches in the United States of America.[9] The study reports congregations range from as few as seventeen members to more than ten thousand. It is conceivable to believe that many of these churches will have at least one annual event, with the majority of them potentially sponsoring two or more each year.

One of the biggest challenges for any church organizer is to get people to the event. Many clever ways have been devised, only two of which are send an RSVP

---

[8] E. W. Lindner, *Yearbook of American and Canadian Churches* (New York: Abingdon Press, Nashville, 2010).

[9] Houseal, Rich, and Dale Jones. *2010 U.S. Religion Census: Religious Congregations & Membership Study (*Nazarene Publishing House, Lenexa, KS) p. 6

or have giveaways, such as winning merchandise or receiving discount coupons to local businesses. We dream of attracting crowds where there is standing room only, only to have that dream dashed when on the day of the event there are too many empty seats.

One would think that over the years we would have finally gotten planning an event right. That we would understand how to improve the planning process and have created a well-oiled machine that—barring acts of God—would run fairly smoothly. However, the opposite seems true. In general, churches seem to lack the necessary professionalism to plan events. One reason may be the constant change at the core orchestration of the event, as the leadership for planning the event keeps changing. Instead of developing a sense of continuity and familiarity with the planning process, they instead spend a lot of time rehashing and revisiting the same issues from previous years.

Members may shudder at the very idea of having to plan the annual special event again, because they feel a lack of consistency in a systematic planning model. I have been present when members groaned and looked at the person next to them with dismay when the annual event was announced or the call for volunteers was made. You can almost hear them say in a not-so-discreet manner, "Has it been a year already?" "Can't we say it's an annual event, but don't hold it yearly?" Others seem to momentarily regress into a comatose state as memories of the last annual event surfaces. Who can forget when Sister So-and-So was in charge? The memories of tense meetings, role confusion, snickering among members, and backbiting seem so fresh. The frustration of the late-night assembling of registration packets was only matched by the early-morning disassembly of the same packets because someone inserted the wrong program. There were people not showing up as promised or arriving late and leaving early. And who can forget the near all-out brawl between the two new members who, if it weren't for the pastor walking by just in time, would have made headline news in the local paper? Oh, no! You made up your mind then that it would take more than a burning bush, the parting of the Red Sea, or a light from heaven to get you to say, "Here I am, Lord, use me," for *any* event again.

It appears that the only person who is interested in the event is—well, actually no one. The pastor seems to dread having to impose on the congregation once more for their individual time and financial obligation. He too remembers being bombarded with complaints from members not wanting to work together and the conflict and near revolt of some of the membership threatening to leave if a certain chairperson did not step down. Committee leaders find reluctance on the part of members to volunteer. No one wants to fast and pray and then wonder why the event lacked the spiritual anointing they had hoped for. The many details that need to be addressed seem overwhelming. The declining economy has not helped, as many are working with leaner household budgets and members seem to be keeping their wallets and purses closed and zipped, if not left at home on purpose.

The Enemy, with all of his subtlety, has succeeded in making church and religious events appear a chore and not worth all the trouble. Someone asks, "Where are the results of my hard work?" "Where are the new members?" "Where are the financial rewards from the fund-raiser?" Without understanding that we are engaged in a spiritual battle when planning a church or religious event, we will constantly fall prey to the Enemy's devices. Knowing that *any*thing done for the Lord will be met with opposition, we must ready ourselves for the battle that will ensue (Eph. 6:10–12). Know this: God will provide the help you need to succeed and will get you through the difficult times of the planning process (Phil. 4:13). Remember that the event provides a venue for God to speak to His people, encourage and strengthen those who may need His reassurance, and draw the unchurched to Him. Once we realize the event is more important to God than to us, we can step back and let the Holy Spirit do the planning.

How does the Holy Spirit lead us? There is sensitivity to the Spirit that we must have. If all committee members strive to walk according to the Spirit and not according to their flesh, seeking God through prayer and supplication, making our requests made known unto Him, He will guide us. Romans 8:1–10 (NIV) says,

> Therefore, there is now no condemnation for those who are in Christ Jesus, because through Christ Jesus the law of the Spirit who gives life has set you free from the law of sin and death. For what the law was powerless to do because it was weakened by the flesh, God did by sending his own Son in the likeness of sinful flesh to be a sin offering. And so he condemned sin in the flesh, in order that the righteous requirement of the law might be fully met in us, who do not live according to the flesh but according to the Spirit. Those who

live according to the flesh have their minds set on what the flesh desires; but those who live in accordance with the Spirit have their minds set on what the Spirit desires. The mind governed by the flesh is death, but the mind governed by the Spirit is life and peace. The mind governed by the flesh is hostile to God; it does not submit to God's law, nor can it do so. Those who are in the realm of the flesh cannot please God. You, however, are not in the realm of the flesh but are in the realm of the Spirit, if indeed the Spirit of God lives in you. And if anyone does not have the Spirit of Christ, they do not belong to Christ. But if Christ is in you, then even though your body is subject to death because of sin, the Spirit gives life because of righteousness.

Six Types of Church and Religious Events

People are drawn to specific churches because the church's ministry, in one way or another, addresses one of their fundamental needs. The church recognizes them as members: they are on the church's membership roll, they give their tithes and offerings, and they attend church activities at least four or more times a month. For them, events for the congregation are very important, as they help to build a community and keep members engaged in the church as a family unit (Ps. 68:6). There are six types of events in the church that serve a specific purpose in meeting their needs. These event goals are not for reaching the unchurched, as these people have already committed themselves and joined the particular church. Rather, the events demonstrate the church's concern for their spiritual maturity and sustainability in the House of God.

Events with defined goals help to:

1. *Strengthen the body of believers.* This type of event provides spiritual development programs to edify the members and to help them grow into spiritual maturity. Such events may include women's or men's conferences or spiritual warfare seminars (spiritual development programs such as specific ministry services and programs).

2. *Conduct organizational business.* Events of this nature provide broad-stroke training experiences for ministry leaders (auxiliary/organization meetings, train-the-trainer, and minister-development workshops).

3. *Communicate/exchange new ideas.* The goal of this type of event is to provide specific information so that individuals within ministries are up-to-date on the latest equipment, services, and resources (teacher conferences and leaders/workers conferences).

4. *Provide resource sharing.* The goal of this event is to present new resources and information to a targeted audience. It may take the form of a resource fair, exhibition teacher, or leadership training. These meetings provide opportunity to network with other individuals or organizations with like interests (singles ministries and women's/men's ministries).

5. *Celebrate milestones.* These events help to create a special kinship or relationship to the church (birthdays and church and pastoral anniversaries).

6. *Fund-raise.* These events have a specific purpose to raise funds for a special cause. These events have a financial goal and can last a few weeks or several years (scholarship and building-fund programs).

Additionally, these goals do not have to be done individually, as some can be combined to accomplish multiple goals. For example, a women's conference can address goals in numbers 1, 4, and even 6. But it would be better that a church anniversary service address only number 5. If you combine an event like this with the other goals, it can appear that you are doing too much. In contrast, larger church or national conferences, particularly those held over several days, can easily address all five or six goals through multiple avenues, such as preaching services, workshops, vendor exhibits, and so on. However, the more goals that are combined, the more work, time, resources, and people will be needed in the planning.

Before you begin planning, and even all along the way, seek God for direction for the event *He* wants for His people. Through prayer, we may find that the unsettling in our spirits is not what an event can cure, but rather it is God's desire to gather the church members together for a time of consecrated prayer, fasting, and seeking Him. The planning of the event is a wonderful way to get people to work together. We get to know others on a personal level. "Behold, how good it is for brethren to dwell together in unity" (Ps. 133:1). Working side by side for anything for God is a powerful force. You can feel His presence right in the mix! Let the Holy Spirit guide you, don't worry, trust Him, and everything will be okay.

Deliverance from Worry

As a child, I worried about anything and everything! I developed stomach ulcers from worrying. I had sleepless nights from worrying. I found worrying to be a normal part of my psyche. Later in life, when I began planning events, my worrying worsened. Thinking about all the things that might go wrong or could go wrong was so heavy on my mind. How liberating it was to learn that Jesus is my burden lifter! I learned to put my trust in Him and let Him be concerned with all of the what-ifs. Now, when the Enemy tries to raise his head (and he will) and throw his weapon of worry into my mind, I go to God seeking His help and peace. I trust the Holy Spirit will alert me to what needs to be done. I wake each morning with a confidence that everything will be all right. What a big relief in knowing there is somewhere more than my own thoughts where I can go—I can go to God in prayer!

Scriptures

"Trust in the Lord with all of your heart and lean not unto your own understanding. In all your ways acknowledge him and he shall direct thy paths" (Prov. 3:5).

"Wherefore let him that thinketh he standeth take heed lest he fall" (1 Cor. 10:12).

"Great peace have they which love thy law: and nothing shall offend them" (Ps. 119:165).

CHAPTER 3

OUTREACH (THE "1")

"The fruit of the righteous is a tree of life; and he that winneth souls is wise."
—Proverbs 11:30

Right Event to Attract Participants (R.E.A.P.)

Who are the *unchurched?* They represent people who do not have a church home and may attend a church once or twice a year at the most. They may show up on special days, such as Christmas, New Year's Eve, Easter, Mother's Day, Father's Day, or other special events, such as a Family and Friends Day. They are not committed to any church. Yet they feel some kind of obligation to attend church at least on one of these special holidays. They are going to attend a church. Why not yours? Let's go fishing!

I remember going on a camping trip one year with my large extended family. One ritual was that the men of the family got up early in the morning and gathered at the dock to catch fish. Before dawn, you could hear them stirring around the cabin. As if unaware that the rest of us were still asleep, their conversation was alive with a sense of urgency and purpose. Chattering, they would boast who was going to catch the most fish, reminding each other of the last outing and results of their efforts. They would grab their premade sandwiches from the fridge, exit the house in a swell of laughter, and drive or walk to the dock. Me? I would wake around noon, casually get dressed, eat breakfast, watch TV, and then nonchalantly walk to the dock to see their progress and how much fish I would be eating that night.

I remember one time wanting to try my hand at catching fish. I grabbed a fishing rod, put—well, had someone else put—the live minnow on the hook, threw the line over the rail, and started talking to the person next to me. Nothing. I waited about two or three minutes, pulled the line back, and threw it out again. Nothing. After a while, I felt a pull on the line. With the strength of Gabriel the angel, I reeled in my line—only to find nothing on the hook. Something nibbled at the bait but did not give enough of itself to get hooked. I blamed my botched attempt on everything: the guys caught all the good fish, I needed professional training, women could not throw the line out as far as the guys since we are the weaker sex, and so on.

After ranting for a few minutes about how fishing was hog posh, one of my relatives came over to see what I was doing. I learned four important points in that conversation: 1) I was making it too complicated. 2) Use the right bait. 3) Have some patience. 4) Wait until the fish get a good bite on the hook before you reel 'em in.

The Bible tells us that we are fishers of men (Matt. 4:19). Experienced fishers are very strategic in *how* they catch fish. One fisherman wrote,

> Fishing is very easy to over-think. Keep it simple. Approach each problem, no matter how complex it may seem, with the attitude that there are always simple solutions. Keeping fishing simple can be one of the most difficult things to do. With the real facts and information, intertwined with advertising and myths, recognizing these true, simple facts can be a major challenge.
>
> Separating facts from advertising, myths, and information designed only to sell products is simple. You must approach each piece of fishing information armed with one fact: fish don't think or make decisions. Fish react to an action. Understanding this, fishing can become quite simple, and the information that can make a real difference becomes quite clear.[10]

---

[10] M. McClelland, "How Do I Become A Better Fisherman?" *Walleye Central*: *http://www.walleyecentral.com/articles/?a=7*.

Just as there were plenty of fish hanging around that dock that day, there are plenty of the unchurched—right in your neighborhood, your family, your jobsite, the mall! They are looking for God, needing God in their lives, wanting a change from the sad routine of their existence. But we have to get them on the hook.

The Bible tells us to be wise as serpents and harmless as doves (Matt. 10:16). If we are to attract the unchurched, we have to assess our strategies. An event is just *one* strategy how to get people to your church, but it should not be a substitute for the Bible's most effective tool—witnessing. You could use the opportunity to tell someone about the event as a segue to witness to them as well. I have found that while it may be difficult to invite some people to a regular Sunday church service or Bible class, you may find them more willing to attend the noncommittal event instead.

Now, since you know they are hanging around your dock (church), you have to set the right bait. I call this process R.E.A.P., which means the *Right Event to Attract Participants*. The *right* event. This is why we have to pray and seek God's direction. Only God knows their needs, hopes, fears, and desires. He has orchestrated circumstances in their lives that will make them receptive to His calling. Your event could be His invitation, the point where they finally surrender to His will. When we seek His guidance in the planning, we are humbling ourselves to His will. We acknowledge that we do not know what to do for His people and seek His help. This then allows the Holy Spirit to help plan the type of event they need.

Remember that events allow people to observe your church without being committed or showing a real interest in your faith. For them, it's *safe*. An example is a church in the Midwest that wanted to get the unchurched through the door and noticed that there were fewer and fewer craft shows in the local area, despite the number of people who made their own wares. They began organizing a craft show for members of their community. As visitors entered the door, greeters presented them with a handout listing the vendors participating in the craft show. However, conveniently tucked in the middle was a beautiful church brochure. Vendors also found a copy of the craft show guidelines and a church brochure at their booths.

Look around in your neighborhood and your city. Is there a need for an activity that your church can sponsor? Simply ask, *"What is a need that we can address through an event?"*

Fundamentally, everyone has needs, wants, hopes, and values. Your church, as a unit, also has needs, wants, hopes, and values. When aspects of these overlap, that is called the sweet spot. Folks are more concerned about themselves than about you. They are more concerned about their issues than yours. It does not matter if the speaker at your event is world-renowned, known for rocking heaven, and his words are like gold nuggets dripping from God. If that wonderful speaker cannot meet a specific need, want, hope, or value, participants may not attend the event. More about the sweet spot will be explained in Chapter 9.

Think about your church. What is your ministry? Do you have a niche? What separates you from the church, not down the street, but right next door? If a church operationally is like a business, then we have to understand how people think and act if we want to attract them to our business. As stated earlier in this chapter, there are potentially hundreds of thousands of events that occur each year. You will find that people are very selective in which event they will attend—whether right next door or half a state away. In this sense, having a variety of ministry programs is good in order to provide several offerings.

Keep the Devil out. Have you ever heard, "We have always done it this way." "Don't mess with something that's not broken." Sound familiar? Oftentimes, organizers will fall into the routine of planning the annual event the same way year after year because *they* think it is working. They believe that because people give compliments it must be okay. There was even significant attendance. So why change it? But is God satisfied? Is your event trying to be all things to all people? Don't try a one size fits all for your events. Don't allow the Devil to persuade you to do the same thing over and over. Prayer should not be a substitute for lack of planning only to hope that God will look past our lackadaisical attitude and bless the event anyway. God is so creative! Let Him give you the fresh, new ideas that can spark a renewed interest in an old event.

Your Event Is an Extension of Your Church's Ministry

A few ministries have been able to identify their niche within the church market and become quite popular. Once they identified *who they were*, they then built *what they were* and then promoted that *message to others*. Take, for example, T. D. Jakes. His "Woman, Thou Art Loose" series hit the sweet spot with women who were hurting or abused and felt abandoned. Those four words launched a ministry of deliverance and faith for many women. From that concept, he conducted conferences, aired a television ministry, wrote books, and recorded CDs and DVDs. His one message was deliverance—but dispersed in different ways.

Take a moment and think about your church by considering several factors. Geographically, what challenges do you have if your church is located in a rural setting? Is it an urban community? Near a university or college? What is the makeup of your community within a three- to five-mile radius of your church? True, years ago, churches were built for people in the neighborhoods, those surrounding their immediate vicinity. Today, people will travel much farther if they enjoy the church's ministry. How might your church's event be impacted by where it is located?

Now, think about the event's purpose and your targeted audience. While there are some events where we may want everyone in the world to attend (e.g., church groundbreakings, pastoral/church anniversary services), there are other events that are designed specifically for certain groups.

If your event is a women's or men's retreat, whom within that category are you trying to reach? All women? All men? Such a goal is ambitious and a daunting challenge. How would you be able to address each person's specific needs? Just considering women and men in general, the following chart shows how these two groups can be further broken down:

Women		Men	
Single Women		Single Men	
Ages 20–34, 35–50, older?	Mothers: never married/divorced with children? Widow?	Ages 20–34, 35–50, older?	Fathers: never married/divorced with children? Widower? commitment issues
Married women (childbearing years, seniors, empty nesters)		Married men (provider, children at home, seniors, empty nesters)	
Hurting women (abused, abusive, abandoned, rejected, low-income, low self-esteem)		Hurting men (abused, abusive, rejected, low self-esteem, ex-convicts, viewers of pornography, covetous)	
Career women/entrepreneurs (new business owners, seasoned owners)		Career men/entrepreneurs (new business owners, seasoned owners)	
Women's health (breast cancer, weight control, menopause)		Men's health (prostate cancer, weight control)	

You see how you could have an event that addresses any of these special interests? And the list can go on. However, there are two things that are common with each person in these groups:

1. God is ultimately concerned about the salvation of each soul and His desire for them to know Him personally in the power of His resurrection and saving grace.
2. Each person is selfish and concerned about one thing in general—himself or herself. Each has what I call the WIIFM syndrome—*What's in It for Me?* (See Chapter 9)

Chameleon Effect

If we walk in the shoes of the unchurched, we can get a better sense of their feelings and thoughts. Have you ever been somewhere, but you really did not want to be there? Or been seeking something, not sure what you are looking for, but think you will know it once you find it? Essentially, that is the experience for many who are the unchurched. People have a myriad of reasons why they do not have a church home. Some may have had a bad experience in their introduction to the church, or they believe God is responsible for some traumatic event in their lives or not answering a prayer. There are a variety of other issues. For many, the pressure of not being a member makes it difficult for them to attend a regular Sunday-morning church service. When an unchurched person does attend a service, we should make it a pleasant experience that he or she will long remember.

What might someone be looking for (consciously or not) when he or she visits?

- Friendliness and warmth
- Genuine welcome, true Christian hospitality
- Effective, well-delivered Bible-based main teaching
- Music deepening the worship, not just entertainment.[11]

---

[11] C. Thompson, *Shocking Beliefs of the Unchurched*. Posted on the *Anchorage Daily News* website November 30, 2008: http://community.adn.com/node/135135#ixzz1Ub240Uiz.

Keep the Devil out. Make every visitor's visit memorable, not miserable. I remember visiting a church service on Mother's Day when I was out of town. The minister criticized those who came to church for that one day but were not regular attendees. You could feel the tension in the room! I understood his motive. It was honorable. He wanted to express that people should not attend services just on a special day, but have a regular relationship with God by attending church more often. However, his tone was so condescending, I even became offended. Instead of making the unchurched uncomfortably stand out, have members go around and welcome them warmly to the service. They could have gone somewhere else. Think to yourself, *If I only have one chance to reach you this year, I am going to make the most of that interaction so that you will want more of our love and hospitality.*

PART 2

NOTHING BY ACCIDENT

"Seest thou a man diligent in his business? He shall stand before kings;
he shall not stand before mean men."
—Proverbs 22:29

Dear Lord,

I bless Your name, my Savior and King! With humbleness of heart, I thank You for allowing me this opportunity to plan this event. It is truly a privilege and honor to be used by You. Please direct my every step and guide my every thought. Let the thoughts that I think be Your thoughts and the words that I say be Your words. Let me not get caught up with worrying about those things that I have no control over. Help me to be mindful and diligent to those things that I should be mindful about. Keep me from the Evil One and help me to be wise to his devices.

I ask for Your strength, wisdom, patience, and understanding. Help me to consider Your desire for Your people. I pray to do my very best, to not seek my glory, but that You will be glorified all along the way. When my heart is overwhelmed, lead me to the rock that is higher than I. I can do all things through Christ, which strengthens me (Phil. 4:13).

Lord, what a wonderful Savior You are! You help us in so many ways to understand those things that are beyond our human capability.

Amen.

CHAPTER 4

MANAGE THE EXPERIENCE:
DON'T HOPE FOR IT ... PLAN FOR IT!

'This is the Lord's doing; it is marvelous in our eyes."
—Psalm 118:23

Keep 'Em Hooked from Beginning to End

Many definitions are given for the word *manage*. However, for the purpose of this chapter, I like the one found in the online Merriam-Webster dictionary: *"to work upon or try to alter for a purpose."* What do we want to manage? The participant's experience of the event: before, during, and after. Julie Rutherford Silvers, CSEP, explains the importance of packaging and managing the participants experience from beginning to end.[12] She attests that, and I agree, we have to think about the participant's experience well in advance of the big day. We must work to create an experience that will cause the event to linger in a person's mind for weeks, months, or even years. In so doing, you could be planting a seed that may, over time, grow into that person's desire to come back to your church—this time to become a member. Using Julie's tool as a starting point, we can modify her ideas to fit a church event:

1. *Anointing*: This isn't one of Julie's recommendations, but one that certainly should be obvious to us who plan church-related events. We need to seek the anointing of God well before the first publicity is sent. Praying and sometimes even fasting to get our Lord's help is important, as souls are at stake.

---

[12] Julie Rutherford Silvers, *Package and Manage an Experience by Mastering the A's of Events.*

2. *Expectation*: Remember the saying, "Mind over matter"? While this phrase says that the mind is more powerful than the body (e.g., controlling pain), this also can be used to refer to people attending your event: if the event is not on their minds, it is not going to matter. Think of it this way: imagine you won a vacation to the beautiful island of Bora Bora. Weeks and months before your vacation arrives, you are making all the proper preparations. The time is blocked off on your calendar. You have purchased your airfare and checked out hotel prices. You may even have talked to people to see if anyone knows about the island and could give their recommendation on the best restaurants and tourist attractions. Long before the day and almost every day since the news that you won the trip, you have done something in preparation for the great time you anticipate having. It's on your mind. Your mind is so powerful that you can actually feel yourself on the beach, your toes splashing in the water, the tall beverage in your hand, the sun against your skin! I heard someone say that 80 percent of pleasure is anticipation. We have to get your event on their minds. Here are suggestions to create anticipation for your event:

    a. Create brochures, invitations, posters, e-mails, social networks, and registration materials.

    b. Send multiple mailings. It takes six to seven contacts with someone before he or she really considers what you're saying. Create a slogan or phrase that is catchy.

    c. Keep it simple. Newspaper journalists realize that you don't want people to work at what they are reading, but rather place themselves at the event, the scene, or the game. Write at a fifth-grade level so people can read through it quickly, rather than stumble over words they do not understand.

3. *Arrival*: How long does it take to make a good first impression? Some say ten seconds; others say less than that. The message here is that you only have a very short amount of time. Miss that opportunity, and you may never get the chance again. Take a slow walk through the entrance of the event; look at your surroundings. Does it feel welcoming? Would you want

to come through that entrance? Here are some easy ideas that can be implemented:

a. Decorations/cleanliness—Decorations do not have to be elaborate, just something nice, particularly around specific seasonal events. Cleanliness is important. Have someone walk around to make sure there is no dirt in the corners or small pieces of paper on the floor.

b. Meet and greet—Station greeters at the front door to welcome the visitors to the event. If possible, do not let people wander around by themselves. If there is no one to greet the guests, post signs on where they should go.

c. Signage—Is the room easy to find if this is someone's first time? Where are the restrooms? That is not something you want someone running around looking for!

d. Guides/ushers—Good ol' hospitality never goes out of style. Ask volunteers who have pleasant attitudes.

e. Instructions/maps—The larger/more complicated the building, the more important maps are. If you have winding corridors or are using multiple floors, provide a floor plan.

f. People want to know what you believe in, so don't leave them guessing. Have an overview of the church's doctrine or mission. (This can be in the form of fliers posted on kiosks or bulletin stands at the front door, a short statement in the program, intricately woven into remarks by the emcee or the person who introduces the speaker, or summarized or reiterated during closing remarks.)

g. Have ministers or ministry workers available to explain the salvation process or share information about the church.

h. Be prepared. Have what is referred to as "all things ready" by ensuring there are ample and clean baptism clothes and conference rooms where you can give people information. Make sure they are clean and odor-free.

4. *Atmosphere:* Nothing sets a spiritual atmosphere like prayer! Evoke God's presence by praying in the areas where you will be meeting. I even like

prayer to start in the parking lot! In addition to the spiritual atmosphere, look at your physical space. What can be done to set the tone?

    a. Staging—On the dais or pulpit, use flowers or greenery to enliven the space. Linen should go to the floor (for modesty purposes), or use skirting.

    b. Props—You do not have to buy anything! Look around in other places of the church for what can be borrowed for the event. This applies to artificial or real trees, garlands, and so on. If you are at a hotel, ask to see what items they have on hand.

    c. Flowers—Real flowers are nice, but artificial ones will work in a pinch. I like to purchase nicer, more expensive artificial flowers when they go on sale. If kept properly, they will last for years.

    d. Balloons—If the balloons are not going to be hung, you may need an inflation machine to keep them afloat. Typically, you should use odd numbers when there are smaller bunches/bouquets (3, 5, 7, or 9); larger bouquets, more than ten, can have equal or unequal numbers.

5. *Food Appeal:* In this section, I am considering more than just the way the food is cooked and presented. Think elevations! Think color! Appetite comes from more than just the food itself. It comes from creating the experience also. (See a photo comparison of a table that provides visual interest in "Tools for Success.")

6. *SWAG (Stuff We All Get):* This is a great opportunity to give your guests something to walk away with. What lasting memory do you want them to have? There are many software programs that allow you to create beautiful designs without needing a professional graphic designer. It will take time, though, so give yourself ample time.

    a. Programs—Include important information about the event. Make sure to check spelling.

    b. Souvenirs/mementos—Such items do not have to be purchased. Create bookmarks from special cards with several encouraging Scriptures on them.

    c. Speaker gifts—This can be tricky, because some people believe that if the speaker is getting an honorarium that he or she should not get a gift. But who doesn't like a gift?

    d. Imprinted items—If your budget allows for professionally printed items such as pens, mugs, and so on, then go for it! But have items you think people will need. You wouldn't want to see your specially purchased items left behind.

    e. Flowers—As I stated above, for some events, artificial flowers are acceptable. For others, they really are not. Think about mixing real and artificial pieces to get a nice look.

    f. CDs and DVDs. This can also be a great revenue generator to offset other costs.

7. *Activity:* Create the *wow* factor! The *wow* factor is what the person will remember about your event. Use an element or particular item over and over again to create a theme. Consider other things also, such as a wonderful greeting staff and cleanliness of the facility. These are little things to attend to, but become huge in the eyes of the participant.

Is the Event Worth Having?

God is the primary head for all events in the church. He has stated clearly whose house the church belongs to. As explained in Chapter 1, the event is in *God's* house, the physical place of worship. Therefore, it is important that we seek God for direction in the planning so that He will be pleased with the end result. Just as you would want things to be handled a certain way in your own house, so does God in *His* house.

What does it mean to acknowledge God as it pertains to events? Too often, churches seem to rely on events to do the work that they are too lazy to do (such as not winning souls individually so they have an event to bring in the unchurched). They may have an event because they are anxious that they have not had one in a while. But is the event what God wants? We have to seek Him first. As I stated earlier, we may find that the unsettling in our spirits is not having another event, but rather spending time with God in prayer and fasting.

One of the most important questions we should ask when an idea for the event has been proposed is, "*Why*?" "Why *this* event?" "Why at this *time*?" "*Why* would/should anyone want to come?" Once the why is answered, then subsequent questions such as who, what, where, when, and how will naturally follow.

Scriptures

"To the weak I became weak, to win the weak. I have become all things to all men so that by all possible means I might save some" (1 Cor. 9:22).

"Let the words of my mouth, and the meditation of my heart, be acceptable in thy sight, O LORD, my strength, and my redeemer" (Ps. 19:14).

CHAPTER 5

SETTING THE FOUNDATION OF THE EVENT

"Buy the truth, and sell it not; also wisdom, and
instruction, and understanding."
—Proverbs 23:23

A Good Plan Starts With A Great Foundation

The most important part of any structure is its foundation. This applies to whether you are building a home, a shopping mall, your business, or your spiritual development. The concept of a foundation is also important as it pertains to planning an event.

The steps involved in planning a successful religious event essentially follow all of the steps in any multifaceted project, except for one key ingredient—the event is directed by God. The issue for many of us is how to distinguish if it's God doing the directing or if we are directing God. We have to take a good strong look at what the event is to accomplish. As we talk about setting the stage or understanding the importance of a foundation for an event, let's look at a couple of key elements to put things in perspective.

You as the Event Architect

A job title that I believe best describes our role as an event planner is that of an architect. Architects are instrumental throughout the life of a building or facility project (from planning to occupancy) as they coordinate the ever-essential design team. The parallels are similar:

Architect	Christian Event Planner
Hired by a client	Appointed by pastor or leader
Responsible for creating a design concept that meets the requirements of that client	Responsible for planning an event that meets the needs of the congregation or a specific group
Provides a facility suitable for the required use	Provides an event suitable for the targeted group
Meets with and questions the client (extensively) to ascertain all the requirements and nuances of the planned project	Meets with and questions the pastor or leader to learn what his or her goals are for the event and what is hoped to be accomplished
Delivers a program or brief, which is essential to producing a project that meets all the needs and desires of the owner. It is a guide for the architect in creating the design concept.	Provides a planning overview of the event that details the goals of the event and the expectations of the pastor or leader. It becomes the guide for the event planner in creating the event.

A *foundation* is the basis or groundwork of anything. In nearly all instances, it sets the parameters of how big or small a project will be. The Bible says that a wise builder measures the costs before undertaking a project. While this Scripture is talking about those in the ministry, we also can apply it to how we approach planning an event. Before the first cornerstone is set, pen is put to pad, or the computer software is opened, there has to be an idea of at least what the end goals are.

The architect has to bring into fruition the image or plan that is in the stakeholder's mind, put that on paper, and project how it will be accomplished.

What's on paper becomes reality, or at least a close rendition of it. Since the success of the project hinges on the clarity and preciseness of the blueprint, the architect spends many hours meeting with the critical individuals to address every detail to the nth degree just to ensure that everyone understands the work ahead even before the project begins. The final blueprint will be a clear picture of the entire project, with everyone agreeing that all are on the same page and the same word.

An architect is hired because he or she brings knowledge of how to create an environment and knowledge of how to reflect an environment. If you think about it, there are environments all around us (a home, a shopping mall, the neighborhood store, a church—each has its own environment). An environment can be a single-family home or a shopping mall. The architect considers how the building will reflect those it is trying to attract; he wants to create an environment to entice a person unaware of the goal. He knows that it's not a one size fits all. People are drawn to different styles of homes as well as malls. Architects have to think how every design can be unique and out of the box so people will be satisfied.

An architect is paid to design, create, and give layout instructions. A great architect will learn about the environment and location where the construction will take place. One important question he or she must ask is, "Why are they building this building?" He understands that the "why" determines the "how." For example, building an apartment building for low-income families is very different from building a condo. The location for the building for the low-income families will be in a different location from the condo. The mind-set of the architect must know who the project is going to be for, as well as who has the money for the project. Usually the architect has ideas that don't fit in the budget, which causes disagreements between him or her and whoever is in charge of paying for the project.

However, before the architect puts pencil to draft paper or brings up a design template on the computer, he or she starts first by consulting with the project owner. An architect understands that although he or she has been hired to create the plan, the project ultimately belongs to the owner. The owner knows what he or she wants the finished project to look like. And most importantly, the owner has the authority to make changes, delay, stop, or give the final okay.

A fluid relationship has to be established between the architect and the owner. The first time working with a new client is always the hardest time because the owner and the architect don't know each other. The interpretation of what is written down is a process where the architect synchs with the owner's ideas. The architect has to know what the owner thinks.

This concept applies to churches as well. Too often churches use a one size fits all for their events. They fall into the routine of planning an event the way they have always planned it because *they* think it works. They may use prayer to substitute for the lack of planning, and hope that God will look past their lack of skill and bring the unchurched in anyway. True, prayer is the key to everything we do for God (do all things in prayer), but God also expects excellence (not perfection, but doing the best of our ability). Since the program is God's, before we jump ahead with our plans, we need to check with Him first.

The second element to be considered is the *stakeholder*. The stakeholder is a person, group, organization, or system that affects or can be affected by an organization's actions. This person or entity has a vested interest in the results of the final product. For the purpose of this book, there are many stakeholders: God, the pastor, and the planning committee. But there are others that oftentimes get overlooked: for example, the church members. How might the event affect them? What about the church's national organization? How does having a successful or poorly planned event affect the organization? Even if the church's headquarters is in another state, what might people think about the organization based on what the local church did? The list can go on for stakeholders: the neighborhood, the city, and the state. Stakeholders with decision-making authority may feel they can make changes at any time because they may have to live with the final decision.

There are several factors the architect has to consider. Where would these homes be built? How would the units be built? What products are durable, but not too expensive? Each step along the way, the architect plans accordingly so that the final product meets the satisfaction of those who initially hired him or her.

People are uniquely diverse in personality and style, and they are drawn to different styles of homes, as well as different malls and types of churches, as well as ministries and events. As an architect has to consider how every end design will meet the needs for someone specifically, we as event planners must also consider who the intended person in the audience is for our event.

Your meetings with the client/owner should provide enough information to get clarity on the purpose of the event, as well as the next steps or direction you should go. In your initial meeting with the client/owner, you should establish how he or she prefers to be updated. Whether you're communicating in e-mails or face-to-face, the conversation should be based on their style, not yours.

I remember several years ago I was at a meeting and was asked on the spot to give an overview of an event to my boss and several high-level administrators. Within the first twenty minutes of my spiel covering just the first half hour of the event day, I looked around the boardroom table and saw nearly all of their eyes glazed over. I realized that I was speaking to several people who thought big picture, not nitty-gritty like me. I tortured them with my cross every "T" and dot every "I" approach to an overview.

I learned that day that to keep people engaged and not lose them with too much information, I had to develop a couple of overview strategies: 1) the quick ninety-second big-picture recap and then 2) the longer, more informational review, which still had to be short and sweet—about five to seven minutes. Gone were the days of *come into my world of details and let's frolic here forever.* I had to think about getting the information to the other person the way *the other person* could receive it. If you are detail-oriented like me, we have to remember that while we thrive in the details, believe the sun rises and sets in details, and the meaning of life is in the details, to others it's just too much information. I suggest that you practice the ninety-second overview and the five- to seven-minute overview. Below is an example of how these conversations would be handled.

Sample Ninety-Second Overview

Thursday meeting 10:00 a.m.

Client/Owner: *"So, where are we with the planning of the event?"*

Event Planner: *"Here is an update of where we stand [you hand him/her a sheet of paper with "Update" on it and the day's date]. Things are moving along smoothly, and we're on schedule. All of our speakers have responded except for Sister Rose Hemford from New Hope Community Church. I left another message on her cell phone and at her church. If I don't hear from her by Tuesday, then I recommend we either move ahead with another speaker or rearrange the program to not include her portion. Additionally, as you can see, all the vendors have received an initial call. I am waiting on quotes or callbacks from all of them. They have until Wednesday of next week to respond. At this point, I just need to know from you whether the board has agreed on the revised budget for the conference to include the uniform shirts for all volunteers as was proposed."*

Client/Owner: *"Yes, let's wait until Thursday for Sister Hemford to respond. I want to give her a couple of extra days. I heard she is out of town at a family member's funeral. As for the discussion on the revised budget, I have not had a chance to meet with the board about that matter. We're not meeting until Thursday morning."*

Event Planner: *"Okay on Sister Hemford. Do you want me to place the shirt item on the board meeting agenda with Secretary Smith?"*

Client/Owner: *"Yes, do that. Just to make sure it's not overlooked."*

Event Planner: *"Well, that does it for me unless you have any other items? I can schedule us to meet next Thursday in the afternoon. By then I hope to have heard from Sister Hemford, and you can let me know the result of the shirt decision from the board meeting."*

Client/Owner: *"Sounds good. See you then."*

Sample Five-Minute Meeting

Thursday meeting 10:00 a.m.

Client/Owner: *"So, where are we with the planning of the event?"*

Event Planner: *"Here is an update of where we stand [you hand him/her a sheet of paper with "Update" on it and the day's date]. Things are moving along smoothly, and we're on schedule. All of our speakers have responded except for Sister Rose Hemford from New Hope Community Church. I left another message on her cell phone and at her church. If I don't hear from her by Tuesday, then I recommend we either move ahead with another speaker or rearrange the program to not include her portion. A couple of speakers I have in mind are Sister Laurita Stalks from Complete New Life Church out of Cincinnati, Ohio. She would bring the experience of someone who has spoken on this topic nationally. She has also written a book* **Twice There, Once Removed***, which talks about ... However, there would be an additional charge of airfare and lodging to bring her in. I actually got a chance to hear her speak at Greater Life last October, and she was phenomenal. People really responded to her well. I believe she would have an attraction to the other churches in the area, as the topic is hot at the moment.*

The other speaker I would suggest is Sidney Crawford, Pastor Rudolf Crawford's wife. Now, she I have not heard personally, but have heard good things about her through Sister Rae Mabley and Sister Alice Allen, who were members at her church for a couple of years before their jobs relocated them to our area. Of interest, she brings the administrative side of the topic. She was involved in ensuring the program was managed and the monies were collected, as well as marketing and evaluation. Sidney Crawford is here in state, thus less cost. Plus, if we don't get the registration numbers we're hoping for, it may be better to have a local speaker to avoid additional costs."

Client/Owner: *"I'll leave it to the committee to decide which speaker will be best. But I do want us to be mindful of the budget, so I prefer that we go with someone local. I've seen Pastor Crawford at a couple of state meetings, but have not had a long conversation with him. His wife seems pleasant enough. I will check with my spouse to see if she has more information. Let's wait anyway until Thursday for Sister Hemford to respond. I heard she is out of town at a family member's funeral. If you don't hear from her by Thursday, let's go with someone else. My choice is local."*

Event Planner: *Moving to the second item, we are extending an invitation to six vendors to participate. As proposed, two sell wares such as jewelry and novelties, two sell Christian books, and the last two sell computer software stuff. As noted on the sheet, all the vendors have received an initial call. I am waiting on quotes or callbacks from all of them. They have until Wednesday of next week to respond."*

Client/Owner: *"Sounds good. But what about the clothing vendor?"*

Event Planner: *"He wasn't available. And I measured the space we have allotted for the vendors; putting a seventh vendor in there would make it really tight. If you still want to go with another vendor, we could either eliminate one of the others, which would be awkward since the invitation has gone out, or we could think about having a page in the program where local vendors could take out an ad."*

Client/Owner: *"Ummm, I like the idea of the ads in the program. Follow-up with the committee on that idea, and let me know how much we would get and how successful it would be."*

Event Planner: *"Will do. So, as a final item, at this point I just need to know from you whether the board has agreed on the revised budget for the conference to include the uniform shirts for all volunteers as was proposed. You may remember that we thought having all of the volunteers dressed alike would look more professional and people could easily see who was a member of the church."*

Client/Owner:	*"As for the discussion on the revised budget, I have not had a chance to meet with the board about that matter, and we're not meeting again until Thursday morning."*
Event Planner:	*"Do you want me to place the shirt item on the board meeting agenda with Secretary Smith?"*
Client/Owner:	*"Yes, do that. Just to make sure it's not overlooked."*
Event Planner:	*"Well, that does it for me unless you have any other items? I can schedule us to meet next Thursday in the afternoon. By then I hope to have heard from Sister Hemford and will give you an update on the program ads, and you can let me know the result of the shirt decision from the board meeting."*
Client/Owner:	*"Sounds good. See you then."*

As you can see from these two conversations, both are about the same agenda items: speaker, vendors, volunteer shirts. The shorter version gives a quick overview, but the goal is to find out if a decision has been made on the volunteer shirts. The longer version brings to surface more of the complexities of the event and provides options for the client/owner to consider. The architect's skill is to present options to any obstacles, rather than leaving it to the client/owner to figure out. I suggest bringing at least two, or even better three, options for the client/owner to think about. It not only shows that you have been thinking of solutions; it also shows the breadth of information that you possess of other resources.

If you are detail-oriented like me, we need to still step back and look at the event with a big-picture lens. We have to see how things connect and envision the entire event from beginning to end. What will people get from beginning to end—not of the event day, but from the first time they hear about the event to after it is over? The event's success will depend on your ability to orchestrate many aspects of the planning process, many of which will include working with the pastor, leader, committee members, and possibly others in the church or religious group.

It is important that you keep in touch with key planning people. Have them report to you at designated intervals (mark those on the planning time line). Your responsibility is to also keep each person informed of the progress, changes, and problems that any of the other committees may have that will impact their work.

Be open-minded and encourage your team members to report problems when they need help. Of course, the speed of your response will be determined by your ability to anticipate potential problems. When planning spans many months, expect changes as a result of family responsibilities, job transfers, illnesses, and the like. As the event planner, you should be prepared to fill vacancies when they occur.

Taking the Heat

I suspect that one of the reasons people may not like to be in leadership is because they do not want to be in the position of being corrected or reprimanded. I believe that correction is a part of leadership. We cannot, and do not, know it all. I wish I could say that you can do everything so right that you will only get accolades all the time. But that is not the reality. Good leadership means understanding that you will not be right all the time or have the entire vision all the time, but are willing to make changes and go a different direction than you originally thought.

Correction to reach excellence is always necessary. If you are corrected, do not take it personally, even if it was done personally to you. There have been so many times that rightfully and wrongly, I have been chastised. However, it is not what they do to you, but the way you handle that situation that matters to God. *Wilson's Old Testament Word Studies* points out that there are two words in Hebrew that are translated as "chastisement." One as *punishment, chastening;* and the other as *to discipline, to correct, to chasten.*[13] *Chastening*, in the tense I am presenting, is discipline and instruction, both done with the care of a loving and benevolent parent. Chastening has as its objective the welfare of the person being disciplined; it should be seen as positive, not negative. However, it can be a hard pill to swallow if you have pride in your heart.

I remember clearly a situation in my secular job that helped me to realize that I was maturing in Christ. We were planning a large event where we were expecting more than a thousand people to attend. Months before the actual event day, the

---

[13] J. Paton, "Chastisement and the Christian," http://www.eternalsecurity.us/chastisement_and_the_christian.htm.

program had already been set. One part of the program included having organization leaders welcome the audience and invite them to join their g After the leaders' comments, a separate panel would follow to field questions the audience.

Everything was in place; however, two weeks before the event, the eliminated a critical part of the program. I tried to see if the others on the pro could fill the gap and met with some of the organization leaders. At that time, of them felt comfortable enough with the potential questions that could come the audience. In the rush of finalizing details, I did not speak to my supervis my boss with this addition. I went ahead, believing it would work out fine bec they were so confident during the meeting.

The day of the event, the boss and a few upper-level administrators we the audience. There were no introductions, no setting the stage. The mode asked the panel to come to the stage. They sat down and ... yep, stage fright! E question they answered, "No, I do not know anything about that," "That was r my experience," or "I never heard anything like that." And I think I'm exaggera because most of the responses were just a shake of the head. I looked aroun room. Dead silence. Members of the audience were texting on their phones, some were even sleeping!

After the event, I received a letter, no, two disciplinary letters that went my personnel file. Why? It was my responsibility to ensure the success of event. My boss and direct supervisor had every right to reprimand me. As I the letter, yes, I cried. The Devil tried to get me to blame the boss for chan; the program at such a late date. However, she had the right to change anyth at the last moment, because it was her event. She owned the event. I was just architect.

I remember praying very hard that evening. I struggled with thoughts the D was bringing to my mind: walk off the job, send her a seething letter, report he her boss. I also could hear the sweet small voice of the Holy Spirit quietly tell me to retain a right attitude, to see how I was held responsible, and to trust F for guidance. The Holy Spirit helped me to realize I was just hurt. My pride v injured. My reputation was spotted. And if I did not handle this properly, my was at risk. When I got to work the next day, I felt I had to send a response. As hands hit the computer keys, this is what God gave me:

Dear (Name),

I am so very sorry for the embarrassment I caused to you at the event yesterday. You were placed in a difficult position having to address the audience after the spectacle of the portion of the event that came before your speech. That must have been very awkward for you, and especially in front of the other administrators. I cannot express how deeply hurt I am that I did this to you. I promise to the best of my ability that this will never happen again. I hope you will find it in your heart to forgive me. I sincerely apologize.

Later that day, I received a response. Not a long one, just a few words: "I accept your apology." That's it. Four words. The main thing was that I was not fired. But I did learn a critical lesson that became a part of my planning process—communicate, communicate, communicate.

Reflecting on the situation objectively, I should have checked with her and my direct supervisor so that we could work through it together. If I had done the Devil's suggestion, I am sure I would not have kept my job. We have to remember that chastisement and correction is not the bad guy. It is not what happens to you, but how you respond. The Bible tells us in Romans 12:17–21 to do what is right and leave the temptation to do revenge in the hands of the Lord:

Recompense to no man evil for evil. Provide things honest in the sight of all men. If it be possible, as much as lieth in you, live peaceably with all men. Dearly beloved, avenge not yourselves, but rather give place unto wrath: for it is written, Vengeance is mine; I will repay, saith the Lord. Therefore if thine Enemy hunger, feed him; if he thirst, give him drink: for in so doing thou shalt heap coals of fire on his head. Be not overcome of evil, but overcome evil with good.

PART 3

WORKING WITH OTHERS

"With all lowliness and meekness, with longsuffering, forbearing one another in love; Endeavouring to keep the unity of the Spirit in the bond of peace ..."
—Ephesians 4:2–3

Dear Lord,

My Lord and Savior, I thank You for Your goodness and Your mercy unto me. Thank You for this day, this opportunity to be used by You to plan this event. Please help me as I work with the people or committee You have given me to plan this event. Please help me to keep my attitude and behavior in the spirit of unity when working with them. Help me to show forth the love of Christ, to keep my spirit in the unity of Your Spirit, to work toward the bond of peace at all times. Let me see something good in each person on my committee. Help me to see their strength and not their faults. Help me to love them as You love them, Your children, the ones You died for and love so dearly. Help me to have the mind of my pastor. Help me to see what You have given him. Increase my understanding. Let me be a help to him, not a hindrance.

Help me to accomplish the goals of this event, *Your* event. May You be pleased in all that I do, that You will get all the glory, all the honor, and all the praise. This I ask in Jesus' name.

Amen.

CHAPTER 6

STRESS IS PAR FOR THE COURSE

"From the end of the earth will I cry unto thee, when my heart
is overwhelmed: lead me to the rock that is higher than I."
—Psalm 61:2

Understanding Your Stress Level

Many people may dread planning an event because of the amount of stress they will endure. The enormous responsibility that comes with ensuring the event will run smoothly, be planned with expertise, have backups for mishaps, and come under budget will create stressful periods. Just thinking about this can cause thoughts of gaining weight and going bald. Whatever your inclination, you will learn a lot about yourself and particularly how you handle stress.

The 2012 CareerCast.com Job Stress Report states that, with a stress score of 49.85, event coordinator landed the number-six spot on the list of most stressful jobs in their annual survey of two hundred different professions that measures work environment, job competitiveness, and risk. An excerpt from that report reads,

> An event coordinator is responsible for planning all logistics and activities associated with the events for which he or she is responsible. Though they may conduct many events through the year, any event may be a once-in-a-lifetime special occasion for the people involved. Therefore, events often have very high visibility and high stakes for the coordinator involved. The top five most stressful jobs all

involve peril and significant hazards. They include Firefighters, who take on dangerous and complex fires, often coming in contact with poisonous gases or other hazardous materials; Airline Pilots, who face potential terrorist attacks and mid-air collisions; Military Generals and Military Soldiers, who are responsible for the lives of many others and often work in hazardous, stressful environments; and Police Officers, who enforce laws and are tasked with catching criminals.

Unsavory individuals? Crisis fires? Mid-planning attacks? Yes, this definitely seems the life of an event coordinator. Bad stress creates the sense of feeling hopelessly overwhelmed. It will immobilize you, paralyze your efforts, and create a most-effective self-defeating attitude. Remember, in times of personal crisis and insecurity, to keep your focus and confidence in your wonderful, loving, and caring Savior, Jesus Christ. When you feel overwhelmed, go to the Rock that is higher than you. I particularly enjoy reading Psalms 145 through 150, as the verses are so spiritually uplifting. These songs remind us of the gentleness of God. "The Lord is gracious, and full of compassion; slow to anger, and of great mercy. The Lord is good to all: and his tender mercies are over all his works" (Ps. 145:8–9). The words seem to lift off the pages and leap into your weary heart. God seems to tell your spirit, "Leave it to Me. Trust in Me. I make things right."

Contrary to what some believe, not all stress is bad. Good stress has its purpose as well. It

- helps you to not approach the event planning casually;
- creates a sense of personal urgency and understanding of the gravity of the responsibility that is placed on your shoulders in ensuring that God's will, the pastor's expectations, the church's/religious group's name, and the participants' needs are met in this one event;
- causes you to pray, and even fast, to seek God's will;
- causes adrenaline to surge through your bloodstream and make you feel excited and enthusiastic at the event;

- provides that sense of challenge and motivation that can take you through difficult times and heighten your awareness and sense of purpose; and
- keeps you ever alert to the devices of the Devil, knowing that he is lurking at all times to disrupt the planning process.

Staff Your Weaknesses

Whether to "staff your weaknesses" or "hire your weaknesses," in both instances, it is basically saying to get help where you lack skill or ability in a particular area. No one is skilled in every area. We have to learn how to identify others who have specific skills that we lack and see if they would be willing to help us fill a skill we lack. For example, if you are not good at writing and you need to send out sponsor letters to generate revenue for your event—ask someone! Nothing can kill a prospective sponsor quicker than a poorly written letter with discombobulated thoughts! And … it's okay. You do not have to be a jack-of-all-trades and master of none. Seek help. Sometimes we let pride get in our way, which is a seed the Enemy is trying to plant to thwart the program. The Bible tells us in Proverbs 16:18 that "pride goeth before destruction and a haughty spirit before a fall." Pride can slip in very easily and when you least expect it. We have to be ever so diligent to pray and ask God whom to go to that can help us. The Bible tells us that we have not because we ask not (James 4:2). God is our help in the time of need! So, you ask, "What are some possible weaknesses where we need to find someone to help us?"

- *Catering.* Cooking, and particularly good cooking, takes training and usually a lot of professional training. As much as you may like cooking in your kitchen, the church-wide event may not be the time to try Aunt Zeta's Italian meatball and mac and cheese strudel. Leave that to your family to enjoy!
- *Graphic design.* Today, with the many software programs that enable people to do their own fliers, many people may feel that they can design the event flier or invitation themselves. However, good graphic design also requires years of training, experimenting, and hands-on experience. Although you create the annual holiday dinner fliers for your job, it may

not be professional enough looking when it has to attract others. What I use to determine if I need to enlist the help of a professional designer for my targeted audience is this: "How will my flier compete with the many other announcements, fliers, and promotions they will receive?" I need my information to look as good as or better than the next thing they get in the mail, handed to them at church, sitting in the flier case, or sent to them via e-mail. You will never have a second chance to make a good first impression. So make that first impression your best—which may require hiring a professional graphic designer.

- *Announcements.* If your church allows time during service for auxiliaries to promote the event and you really don't like speaking in front of people, get someone to make that announcement for you. Everything about the person or people promoting the event *conveys* the event message: his or her tone, attire, excitement level, clarity of speech, and overall look all send a message.

- *Organizing.* God may have given you the overall vision, but an event requires step-by-step execution of a myriad of tasks that need to be managed. If you get lost when trying to systematically arrange things in a sequential order, you will need someone who loves or does well organizing things.

- *Follow-up.* Returning phone calls, sending e-mails, and scheduling or rescheduling meetings are all a part of follow-up. The timeliness of handling these requests is important and cannot be overlooked. When we take a lackadaisical attitude toward returning calls or e-mails, we can inadvertently cause someone to think about us negatively. If you do not check your e-mails on a daily basis or visit your social network sites regularly, you may be missing some very important information. There are people who literally stay connected to their cell phone, tablet, or social network all day! Ask for help with following up on the crucial items.

The Event Planner's Schedule

This chart provides a general overview of the event planner's time line for managing an event from start to finish. It should be held in conjunction with the longer P.E.A.C.E. time line, which is provided in chapter 11. Determine where you might need assistance in following through on any of these responsibilities. In this sample time line the Tasks column provides an overview of your responsibilities from beginning to end. The Countdown column alerts you when things need to happen. In the Notes column, write out what needs to be done for that task.

Tasks	Countdown	Notes
1. Meet with the pastor/client/ leader to determine purpose and goals of the event. (a) Review constraints (scope of the event, budget, time, and their expectations). (b) Present/inquire who may be on committee. (c) Present and review planning time line for each functional area. (d) Inquire about budget.	10	Arrive at an agreement or request another meeting time to hash out any problems/ concerns.
2. Select committee chairpersons and members.	9	Pair people with assignments that accentuate their strengths, not weaknesses.
3. Arrange first planning committee meeting of all pertinent individuals.	9	If you cannot meet physically, try a free conference-call line. It is important to have as many there as possible.

4. Hold first planning meeting. (a) Welcome and introduce those present. (b) Present pastor's/leader's goals and work with committee to discuss additional goals and objectives for the event. (c) Discuss possible sites and dates. (d) Explain purpose and content of planning time line. (e) Distribute the master planning time line to each person. Explain each person's role and review selection of committee members. If you have some committee members' names already, give names to the committee chair. (f) Distribute budget and review. (g) Determine future meeting schedule.	8	Carefully go through the goals and ensure everyone is on the same page. Everyone does not have to agree, but at least everyone should understand the goals. Determine future meeting times with the pastor/client/committee.
5. Monitor progress of each committee's work and oversee planning meetings.	ongoing	This will mean that as the event planner, you will need to follow up with people to see how their tasks are coming along.
6. Manage the big day.	0	Pray and trust God that all the work you and the committee have done will be rewarded.

7. **Evaluate and debrief.**	+1	After the event, meet with the core planning members to review if goals were met. Discuss lessons learned and collect them in folder/electronic file.
8. **Prepare final report.**	+2	Meet with pastor/client/ leader and review final report.

Scriptures

"The Lord shall fight for you, and ye shall hold your peace" (Ex. 14:14).

"The Lord will give strength unto his people; the Lord will bless his people with peace" (Ps. 19:11).

"In all thy ways acknowledge him and he shall direct your paths" (Prov. 3:5–6).

CHAPTER 7

THE POWER OF ONE

"Hear, O Lord, and have mercy upon me: Lord, be thou my helper."
—Psalm 30:10

Going Solo

At some point, you may find yourself planning an event by yourself. Either you dove into the planning fully aware that you were going at it alone, or you found yourself on a committee where the workload has become imbalanced and you are stuck with doing most of the work. Having your spiritual antenna upright is important in both situations. In the former, the Enemy may try to have you doubt your ability for a successful outcome. In the latter, he will try to sow the seed of bitterness toward those who are supposed to be helping and are not.

For the lone planner, certainly the idea of planning an event by yourself has its advantages: all ideas are great—in fact genius, because they are yours! You arrive at your own meetings on time and end when you want to; you can slack off and not get reprimanded (no chastisement here!); you never have to prepare an agenda or take notes; and most of all, you can avoid disagreements! Seems great! Well, why so gloomy? While it may appear that the best way to avoid headaches, confusion, and mayhem is to just do all the work by yourself, it also can become overwhelming. Every event has periods when the steps get combined or start to close in together so quickly that you can feel you do not have enough time to get everything done.

God has designed the human body with mechanisms to inform us when we are stressed. Stress can present itself as fatigue, worry, inability to concentrate, or anxiety. It can manifest itself silently as prolonged procrastination on a particular task, becoming increasingly moody, feeling depressed about the work that lies ahead, or having doubtful thoughts about the event being successful. These internal mechanisms are indicators that should not be ignored.

Stress, particularly for large events, will happen. However, being ignorant of the Devil's devices in the planning can make us vulnerable to his attack. The Enemy will try to make situations worse by orchestrating things and people in order to upset us, to get us off track, to get us to throw in the towel, or to get us to vow never to plan an event or plan an event with *that* person ever again. His intent is to eventually get us to the place where we will complain to God, rather than looking to God for help and support.

Ephesians 6:12 tells us that our fight is not against one another, or what some may believe, against God: "For we wrestle not against flesh and blood, but against principalities, against powers, against the rulers of darkness of this world, against spiritual wickedness in high places." This spiritual wickedness becomes a united evil force that works against every Christian believer. Even when the event does not appear to have an obvious spiritual connection per se (e.g., high school football tailgate), because *you*, the child of God, are planning the event, you will have demonic opposition.

How the Devil tries to accomplish this is found in 1 Peter 5:3: "the adversary the devil, as a roaring lion, walketh about, seeking whom he may devour." One definition for *devour* is to *overwhelm*. When you become overwhelmed, both your mind and emotions are deeply affected. The Enemy will engulf you with demands (both internal and external influences). Some typical ways I have noticed what happens to myself and other people is to become consumed with worry and obsessed with every tiny detail. Away goes the desire for the event to happen, but rather, you just want for the event to end. When you find yourself feeling this way, remember you can cry out to God, who is your refuge, strength, and a very present help in the time of trouble (Ps. 46:1).

Working alone on an event requires discipline and a structure. In chapter 11, I will introduce the Pray/Project/Task Planning Time Line. This tool is the structure you need to keep the planning process moving at a reasonable pace. As you follow the planning time line, you will know if you are falling behind, when and where to direct more time, and when to find additional resources to help you get things done and back on track.

Remember, in all reality, you are not alone. God is with you. He's always with you. He is concerned about everything you do, whether you think it's directly related to Him or not. The Bible assures us that God will never leave us or forsake us (Heb. 13:5). It's hearing His peaceful voice of direction that can be a challenge. When the hustle and bustle of the event planning is in full swing, we need to find quiet mental space to hear God's voice.

Planning an event alone does not have to mean solely by yourself. As I mentioned before, seek help where you can. Ask another member who may have certain skills or gifts to take something off your hands. For instance, ask the church secretary or another member to help create the name badges or signage. Ask people to help with assembling the SWAG (stuff we all get) bags. Whatever way someone can help, helps to reduce something that you have to do. I remember a friend lamenting that she was not able to help me as much as she wanted and that all she did was create the name badges and pick up the balloons from the store. I told her, "You may not have given in volume, but what you did was significant. Thank you."

Keep the Devil out. The Devil is counting on the possibility that you do not know the voice of God well enough to distinguish it from his. He mixes a daily concoction of deception and lack of scriptural understanding with a dose of twisting the truth to produce confusion and self-doubt in the mind of the child of God. Keep him out! To counteract his attack, find some Scriptures that will get you through those trying times when the Enemy seems to be launching an all-out attack on you and your event. A few Scriptures that really helped me are:

"For God hath not given us the spirit of fear; but of power, and of love, and of a sound mind" (2 Tim. 1:7).

"Knowing this, that the trying of your faith worketh patience. But let patience have her perfect work, that ye may be perfect, and entire, wanting nothing. If any of you lack wisdom, let him ask of God that giveth to all men liberally, and upbraideth not; and it shall be given unto him" (James 1:3–4).

"I had fainted, unless I had believed to see the goodness of the Lord in the land of the living. Wait on the Lord: be of good courage, and He shall strengthen thine heart: wait I say, on the Lord" (Ps. 27:13–14).

One as Collective Power

The Old Testament shares the story of when the Lord instructed Moses to take the sum of all the congregation of the children of Israel and number them according to their families (Num. 1:2). Some of these groupings were well into the thousands (Num. 2:4). The Levites also were numbered before the Lord before they could minister in the priestly offices (Num. 3:15). The importance of numbering continues in the New Testament, as we see that Jesus chose twelve apostles (Luke 9:1–2) and later another seventy others as His own (Luke 10:12). More than five hundred brethren saw Jesus in His ascension (1 Cor. 15:3–6). Before Pentecost, 120 disciples were gathered in the upper room (Acts 1:15), and since the day of Pentecost, millions have come to Christ as their Lord and Savior. However, there is a number that carries special significance, the number *one*.

The Bible mentions this three-letter word just 1,697 times. The *One* is revealed to Israel in the Old Testament: "Hear, O Isra-el: The Lord our God is *one* Lord" (Deut. 6:4); and in the New Testament, Jesus acknowledges to the Jews, "I and my Father are *One*" (John 10:30). We learn there is but "one lord, one faith, one baptism, One God and Father of all, who is above all, and through all, and in you all" (Eph. 4:5–6).

Furthermore, the Bible explains that the church is one body working together (1 Cor. 12:12–17). *One* is also used as a definition for *unity*. The synergy of a few people working together on a common cause is much more powerful than fifty people divided by their own opinions. When we work together on one accord, we are much stronger together than trying to handle things by ourselves. There is a great example in Genesis 11:1–9 (NRSV) that demonstrates what happens when the people come together with one mind to accomplish a task. Their determination drew even God's attention:

> Now the whole earth had one language and few words. And as men migrated from the east, they found a plain in the land of Shinar and settled there. And they said to one another, "Come, let us make bricks, and burn them thoroughly." And they had brick for stone, and bitumen for mortar. Then they said, "Come, let us build ourselves a city, and a tower with its top in the heavens, and let us make a name for ourselves, lest we be scattered abroad upon the face of the whole earth." And the LORD came down to see the city and the tower, which the sons of men had built. And the LORD said, "Behold, they are one people, and they have all one language; and this is only the beginning of what they will do; and nothing that they propose to do will now be impossible for them. Come, let us go down, and there confuse their language, that they may not understand one another's speech." So the LORD scattered them abroad from there over the face of all the earth and they left off building the city. Therefore its name was called Ba'bel, because there the LORD confused the language of all the earth; and from there the LORD scattered them abroad over the face of all the earth.

One person had an idea that reached a state of such confidence that he was able to instill that confidence in someone else. Together, they believed in each other. And together they got others to believe the impossible too. What seemed impossible to some was a possibility to them. Without having the technology, equipment, and machinery we think would be necessary to accomplish such a project, they did with far fewer resources. Build a tower to heaven? Even such an idea being presented to us today would cause us to laugh and call it preposterous. Some may even recommend spiritual intervention and psychiatric treatment for someone having such a foolish thought today. Continuing such unwanted conversation may lead some to report the person to the spiritual leader with the suggestion that he or she be quickly removed from all positions before others are swayed to such outlandish thinking.

Working together should not be a mystery or misery for the body of Christ. Why does it seem the Devil works harder at stopping us from the work of the Lord than we do at keeping the work going until the job is finished? The Devil needs not to use tangible objects such as stone and mortar; rather, he builds with the seeds of resentment, discord, and disagreement among those who are part of the program. He causes non-supporters to criticize the workers' efforts, disagree with their ideas, gossip about them behind their backs, miss scheduled meetings, and if they do attend a meeting, come unprepared. Yes, the story in Genesis 11 illustrates what determination is ... it keeps you on target despite the opposition.

Although this story depicts a time in Israel's history when men acted of their own accord to build the Tower of Babel, can you imagine what they would have accomplished if God were working with them? Each person had a role and understood his or her assignment. For that moment, Israel got it—that their greatest resource was each other, and that together they could accomplish a monumental dream.

Keep the Devil out. I remember when my daughter was a teenager and she was rebelling against certain rules I had established in the house. She would become very upset with me, complaining that I was not agreeing with her after she had laid out the points to her argument. She would say, "Mom, you're not listening!" I explained that I was *listening*, but I was not *agreeing* with her. She felt that if I listened long enough, she would eventually get me to agree. But that was not the case. We can often feel that someone is not listening to us if he or she does not side with us. How can we work together so that our disagreements do not cause division? The Devil brings confusion and every evil work. If such is happening, step back and ask God to send peace and harmony, as demonstrated in Romans 12:9–16:

> Let love be without dissimulation. Abhor that which is evil; cleave to that which is good. Be kindly affectioned one to another with brotherly love; in honour preferring one another; Not slothful in business; fervent in spirit; serving the Lord; Rejoicing in hope; patient in tribulation; continuing instant in prayer; Distributing to the necessity of saints; given to hospitality. Bless them which persecute you: bless, and curse not. Rejoice with them that do rejoice, and weep with them that weep. Be of the same mind one toward another. Mind not high things, but condescend to men of low estate. Be not wise in your own conceits.

CHAPTER 8

WORKING WITH OTHERS

"Iron sharpeneth iron; so a man sharpeneth the countenance of his friend."
—Proverbs 27:17

Working with the Pastor or Client

The client or stakeholder of the project could be the pastor, associate pastor, the director, or someone who is simply in charge. The event planner's job is to get into the mind of the client. If the client is having difficulty clearly explaining what he or she wants as the objective and end result of the event, remember that God, as the ultimate owner of every spiritual event, does have an end goal—souls. So you can always ask Him the question: will this event strengthen the body of Christ? Will it cause the members to be edified, or the unchurched to convert to Christ?

More often than sometimes, it will take prayer, research, and studying to understand the mind-set of the pastor or client. As you begin to pray and diligently seek the Lord for direction, you will see a metamorphosis begin to happen: the event becomes yours too. You will find yourself beginning to think about it all the time. You will find yourself in conversations with church members or those outside the church who you will discover can be helpful in carrying out an aspect of the tasks. The event will start to come together in your mind. You may not have an absolutely clear picture, but something will start to form.

The event will begin to take on such importance to you that it may be hard to understand why the event is not the top priority of everyone's mind: your pastor, the leaders, and the congregation.

I suggest that you establish with the pastor/client/leader when to meet, how often to meet, and his or her preferred way to be contacted. How you do this will be based on the temperament or personality of the person. How he or she prefers updates will need to be discussed and mutually agreed upon between the two of you. For example, if you and, let's say, the pastor agree that you can call him or her anytime to address an issue, three o'clock in the morning may not be his or her idea of "anytime." Today's advanced technology does not always mean that e-mail is the best method to communicate. In fact, there are studies suggesting that people still prefer face time at some point. If it is geographically impossible to meet, try Skype, FaceTime, or some other visual way of connecting.

Architects understand that although they have been hired to create the plan, the project ultimately belongs to the client. The architect's goal is to establish a fluid relationship between himself or herself and the client. The more they understand each other, the better the end result will be. I believe there can be unintentional misunderstandings when our role changes so that we are no longer just a member of the congregation but now the architect/event planner of the event. Even though you may have been going to your church for years, counseled with the pastor, and spoken to him regularly, once you take the lead on planning an event, the relationship changes. Now you have to establish a new relationship with the pastor/client.

Working with him or her this first time in this capacity will take an initial conversation and may need ongoing meetings to build confidence in both parties. Just like you have to get to know the mind of your pastor in this new way, equally your pastor has to get to know the way you think. Do you think like him or her? Are your goals the same? What comes out of your mouth in your meetings will either build that confidence or cause his or her knees to shake. The more you work together, the more you will begin to understand each other. Regular meetings and even casual conversations help to reveal idiosyncrasies, communication styles, and lifestyles. I have heard that some event planners know their pastors so well that the pastor does not have to say words for them to understand what he or she wants.

In the end, what went well or not well will be on the shoulders of the pastor. It is therefore our responsibility to keep him or her in the loop. I call it the no-surprise rule. Once you establish the best way the pastor prefers to be contacted, you can simply update him or her on critical decision points from the previous meeting. For example, when I was asked to oversee the planning of a large weeklong event, I met with my pastor initially to get his goals and expectations. In all of our subsequent meetings, I could simply detail the current status of efforts toward his goals and expectations.

Is the Holy Spirit in the Midst?

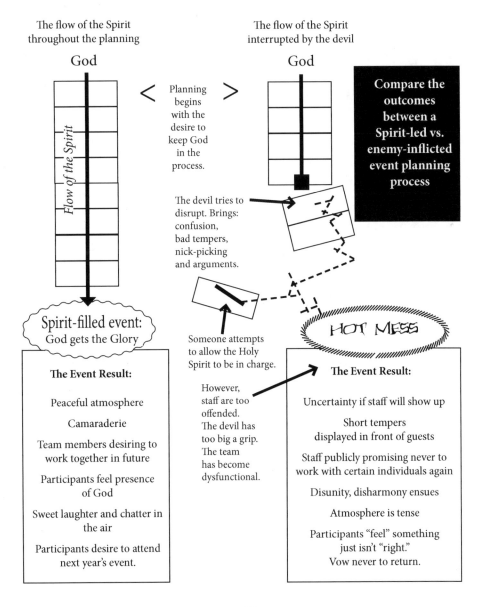

The flow of the Spirit throughout the planning

The flow of the Spirit interrupted by the devil

God

God

Flow of the Spirit

Planning begins with the desire to keep God in the process.

Compare the outcomes between a Spirit-led vs. enemy-inflicted event planning process

The devil tries to disrupt. Brings: confusion, bad tempers, nick-picking and arguments.

Spirit-filled event:
God gets the Glory

HOT MESS

Someone attempts to allow the Holy Spirit to be in charge.

However, staff are too offended. The devil has too big a grip. The team has become dysfunctional.

The Event Result:

Peaceful atmosphere

Camaraderie

Team members desiring to work together in future

Participants feel presence of God

Sweet laughter and chatter in the air

Participants desire to attend next year's event.

The Event Result:

Uncertainty if staff will show up

Short tempers displayed in front of guests

Staff publicly promising never to work with certain individuals again

Disunity, disharmony ensues

Atmosphere is tense

Participants "feel" something just isn't "right."
Vow never to return.

The diagrams illustrate the difference between two groups planning an event. The first shows what happens when God is in control. Committee members experience peace in the planning and camaraderie among themselves. More importantly, the recipients of that peaceful planning feel the presence of the Lord at the event. In contrast, the second illustration shows what happens when the devil has crept into the planning process. The enemy brings confusion, discord, infighting and contention. The result of his handy work affects not only the planners, but also the unfortunate participants who experience an event where the presence of the Lord is stifled or absent.

Working with Committees

The Bible tells us in Ecclesiastes 4:9 that, "Two are better than one because they have a good reward for their labour. For if they fall, the one will lift up his fellow: but woe to him that is alone when he falleth: for he hath not another to help him."

I heard a faculty member say one time; "Two heads are better than one—even if one is a goat head!" Certainly this does not mean that someone is less smart than you. It simply could mean that he or she may not have all the skill and expertise you do, but what he or she does have can be very helpful. Learning to delegate without micromanaging will cause people to want to work with you. Do not be tempted to jump in and turn someone's idea into your way of thinking. Sometimes I may have done something different, and it may have looked even more professional. But that was not important. The fact that it was done helps. The fact that I do not have to worry about doing that thing helps even more.

> I therefore, the prisoner of the Lord, beseech you that ye walk worthy of the vocation wherewith ye are called, With all lowliness and meekness, with longsuffering, forbearing one another in love; Endeavoring to keep the unity of the Spirit in the bond of peace. (Rom. 4:1–3)

It may seem impossible to follow this Scripture at times—to work peacefully with all people. In reality, some people are extremely difficult to work with. However, it is God's expectation that we would work together in the bond of peace. Can you imagine how frustrated God must be with us at times? He has declared that His thoughts are not our thoughts and His ways not our ways. It does not matter how much we want Him to understand that my ugly behavior was the result of someone else's doing. God measures our maturity in Him by the way we conduct ourselves and the way we treat those who wrong us, persecute us, and say all manner of evil against us (Matt. 5:11).

True, there are some people who can really make you wonder if it is worth the hassle of chairing the event committee for all the trouble they are causing you. You may begin to wonder what God could have possibly been thinking when He put you in such a position. It has caused you to get so angry and frustrated with people who are so unlike you. There seems to be so much bickering and noncompliance from those on the committee. But that sounds like something God would definitely do! You may want to give that person a piece of your mind. Don't do it! You are going to need *your entire mind* to get through the planning process!

I remember when I was asked to lead the planning for a large multiday conference for the church. One of the tasks that I had to follow up on with the planning committee after meeting with the pastor was whether volunteers would purchase coordinating shirts so we all could be uniformed. The pastor wanted the shirts; however, he did not want to place a financial burden on the volunteers. When I met with the committee and brought up the idea of the shirts, people were unenthusiastic because they too were concerned about the cost to the volunteers.

Both the pastor and the committee had the same concern—cost. However, as architect, it was my job to come up with the options—the *how* to make it happen. A lengthy discussion about the price of the shirts ensued. I kept taking us back to the wishes of the pastor that he wanted shirts for the volunteers. So, if price were not an issue, what would the shirts look like? What would the color be? Would all subcommittees have the same color? Did we want T-shirts or dress shirts?

Was it important to add cost considerations at this time? No, what we needed was a flow of ideas. Then, after several minutes of throwing out great ideas, I asked if people *did* pay for their own shirts, particularly since the committee agreed that they wanted the nicer dress shirt, how much would they be willing to pay? More discussion! That was my goal. I wanted the committee to talk about possibilities, not improbabilities. It's easy to get caught up in negative talking, but such conversation has defeating purposes. The Scripture reminds us that we can do all things through Christ, which strengthens us, and only without God are all things impossible.

As the conversation's atmosphere changed, ideas were flowing, and then there was a spirit of unity, working toward one goal—yes, let's get the shirts!

After we agreed on a very nominal cost that volunteers would most likely be willing to pay, one of the committee members suggested having a fund-raiser that would offset the rest of the cost for the shirt. Thank You, Jesus! We had the shirts, we had a nominal price for members to pay out of their pocket, we had a fund-raiser to offset the balance, we accomplished meeting the wishes of the pastor, and most of all, we worked together in unity.

In this particular situation, yes, I could have gotten upset and demanded that we do what the pastor wanted. However, that would have drawn some away, if not literally, then in spirit. So, I learned some general principles when working with others:

1. *Be careful of your emotions and those of others on the committee.* Emotions can impair one's ability to think clearly. The angrier someone may be, the harder it is to rationalize with that person. One way to avoid that is to be clear in the expectations of the idea or task. Leave out emotional triggers such as "you people" or "never." Build on possibilities, not negatives. Remember that people are very concerned about three particular things: their families, money, and time. It is the event planner's responsibility to keep them connected to the group.

2. *Be clear in your expectations.* Implicit expectations say, "What didn't you understand about what I didn't say?" Sometimes we think we are making perfect sense, but to others, we may be missing critical information. Can

they repeat back what you were saying, not necessarily in exact words, but the gist should be there? When expectations are clear, it leaves little room for doubt or confusion. People can move confidently forward, knowing what you expect of them.

3. *Work with others without conflict and infighting.* Colossians 3 gives us some concrete ways in which we should work with one another. Oftentimes the bickering and infighting are because we have not mortified our flesh (v. 5). What does mortification look like? Consider road kill. Mortification is when you cannot recognize what the dead animal is; there is no resemblance of what it used to be. Everything about its past is gone. That is how it should be with us. If I still fly off the handle because someone disagrees with me, my flesh is not mortified. If I want to wring someone's neck because I am tired of his or her thwarting of all of my efforts, I am not mortified. If I still feel the tinge of anger rise up in my heart toward anyone, I am not mortified. And if I am not mortified, God is not glorified. The Bible reminds us, "Forbearing one another, and forgiving one another, if any man have a quarrel against any: even as Christ forgave you, so also do ye. And above all these things put on charity, which is the bond of perfectness. And let the peace of God rule in your hearts, to the which also ye are called in one body; and be ye thankful" (Col. 3:13–15).

4. *Do not render evil for evil.* If you stay in your lane and do what's right, God will bless you. Do not get caught up in talking about others on the committee. That is an erosion that is not seen until too late. "And whatsoever ye do, do it heartily, as to the Lord, and not unto men; Knowing that of the Lord ye shall receive the reward of the inheritance: for ye serve the Lord Christ. But he that doeth wrong shall receive for the wrong which he hath done: and there is no respect of persons"(vv. 23–25).

Keep the Devil out. If you are having problems with a particular person, be prayerful and ask God how to address the situation. Do not confront the situation. I do not recommend that things just be left without addressing them, as they may get worse. However, it's the way that you do it that makes the difference. Before approaching the situation in prayer, think if you have done anything. The Bible tells us in Matthew 5:23–24, "Therefore, if thou bring thy gift to the altar, and therefore rememberest that thy brother hath ought [anything] against thee; Leave there thy gift before the altar, and go thy way; first be reconciled to thy brother, and then come and offer thy gift." So, *before* you go to that person, ask God to prepare your heart to make sure it is right first, because you wholeheartedly and humbly want to correct the situation. The Devil will want to use the opportunity to create another issue. Ask God for the time and the place when you should speak with the person and be prayerful so that God will direct your conversation. There is research that purports that there is a psychology to the way people respond to an apology. *The Five Languages of Apology* by Dr. Gary Chapman is an excellent reference on how to approach people in delicate situations such as conflict resolution.

Scriptures

"Depart from evil, and do good; seek peace, and pursue it" (Ps. 34:14).

"I exhort therefore, that, first of all, supplications, prayers, intercessions, and giving of thanks, be made for all men; For kings, and for all that are in authority; that we may lead a quiet and peaceable life in all godliness and honesty" (I Tim. 2:1-2).

PART 4

PLANNING THE EVENT

"Let all things be done decently and in order."
—1 Corinthians 14:40

Dear Lord,

Thank You for Your goodness, mercy, and kindness. Another day in the land of the living, and I give You the praise. I give You glory for the assignment You have given to this committee to plan an event for Your people. Please give us the wisdom and understanding of how to develop an event that will meet each individual and spiritual need. When we seek what Your people need at this event, please help us to create the questions that ask the heart of the matter of things they are concerned about, the things they want to grow in, the challenges to their Christian walk. Give us spiritual insight and understanding into the needs of those who will attend.

Let Your Spirit lead from the beginning to the end. Show Your mighty hand in orchestrating every aspect of this event. Guide our thinking so that we place ourselves in the shoes of the attendees. Help us to be mindful of Your direction. Hold back the works of the Enemy. Help us to be wise to his devices. We give You the glory, honor, and praise. Our desire is to do Your will at all times. Lead us in the way You would have us to go. In Jesus' name.

Amen.

Sample Event

From this point on, we will take a mock event and follow the planning from beginning to end. This is an event to plan the first annual women's conference at your church.

~~~~~~~~~~~~~~~~~

Women's Conference

~~~~~~~~~~~~~~~~~

at
Life Is Meaningful Community Church
Your Town, USA 12345

CHAPTER 9

GETTING STARTED

"The Spirit of the Lord is upon me, because he hath anointed
me to preach the gospel to the poor; he hath sent me to heal the
brokenhearted, to preach deliverance to the captives, and recovering
of sight to the blind, to set at liberty them that are bruised."
—Luke 4:18

Assess Your Audience

Before jumping fully into the planning, we need to get a good idea of what our audience needs. Why spend all that time planning the event only to learn later, and sometimes too late, that the event did not accomplish its original purpose? Remember the chart in Chapter 3? People are not hoping to attend your event because it would make *you* happy. They are attending because the event will meet a *personal* need. Always remember that concerning events, people are selfish, self-motivated, and concerned primarily about one thing—themselves. So, if I'm going to have an event that will attract an audience, I have to first find out what those needs are. This can be done through a needs analysis.

In simplest terms, a needs analysis collects information about your participants' needs, wants, wishes, and desires, as they pertain to their expectations of the event. The process also involves looking at the expectations of other interested parties, such as the pastor, the auxiliary or group leader, administrators, financial supporters, you, and other people who may be impacted by the event (such as other church members, the community, and the church organization). A needs analysis can be very formal, extensive, and time-consuming, or it can be informal, singularly focused, and quick. Some resources for conducting a needs analysis may include surveys and questionnaires, previous evaluations, and interviews.

The information gleaned from the needs analysis will help define the conference goals. These goals can then be stated as specific objectives, which in turn will function as the foundation on which the conference plans, speakers, workshop ideas, and activities will be developed. Basically, a good needs analysis will help you to clarify the purposes of the conference.

How a needs analysis is completed will depend on the situation, who is doing it, and why it is being done. For our Women's Conference, we want to customize the needs analysis to the specific needs of our audience. In order to do this, we need to get the targeted audience's input, opinion, and ideas for speakers, topics, and potential dates and times.

There are several ways to conduct a needs analysis:

1. *Create a survey or questionnaire* (electronic or hard copy). The survey instrument should be developed in such a way that members of your group will actually complete it. For example, some of the younger generation may complete something that has been sent to them electronically, whereas more senior members may want a hard copy to complete.
2. *Convene a focus group* with a representative sampling of your targeted audience.
3. *Have spot interviews* where you randomly stop people and ask for their opinion.

Once some information on your audience has been collected, then take time to study, discuss, and analyze the information:

1. *Study*—Are there similarities between your event and others? Are there lessons learned that should be duplicated or avoided? What does your targeted audience say about their needs? Who is your targeted audience (remember not everyone is a target; see chapter 3 for details)? How will you reach them? Why should they come? Ask, from the participant's perspective, "What's the WIIFM (What's in It for Me)?" Is there a similar event happening

before yours that you can attend to get ideas? You can even research current topics on the web for ideas.

2. *Discuss*—Meet with the owner/client and committee members (this can be done in separate meetings or together) and review the needs analysis. Is everyone on the same page? If not, work through overarching or major issues now. Do not wait until what may seem initially to be a molehill turns into a mountain later. I am not suggesting that you haggle over every minute detail at this time, but at least know what has to be addressed later. Use this time to discuss, in general, the event's goals and objectives.

3. *Analyze*—Take time to examine all of the parts of the event in careful detail, in order to identify causes, key factors, possible results, or essential features. How are things connected? Is there a consistent message or theme emerging from all the input that was received?

Reviewing the needs analysis is a process that is best conducted with more than just one person. Find a time separate from the regular meeting time to discuss your findings. You can also ask a subcommittee to create a summary, thus making it easier and quicker to review responses.

Once you have collected information and have a sense of the direction the Lord is leading you for the event, take a moment to think about the event as a whole. Every event has a life cycle, a starting point, and an end product. The Bible tells us that where there is no vision, the people perish (Prov. 29:18). With every opportunity, the message of the Bible and salvation needs to be conveyed to people. It needs to be done not only in written form, but also audibly. God has a unifying message throughout the entire Bible. This also runs true for the life cycle of your event. Is God in charge throughout?

In summary, all events will have their particular challenges in the planning stages. Whether birthdays, dinners, weddings, or receptions, there are ups and downs of undertaking such a responsibility. The ultimate goal for the church event is to create an experience that will so profoundly impact your guests that they won't soon forget. God is unforgettable. You may ignore Him. But you can't forget Him.

Determine the Sweet Spot

Sweet Spot
Where interests overlap

Church has:
• Needs
• Wants
• Hopes
• Values

Individual has:
• Needs
• Wants
• Hopes
• Values

All of our planning for the event, from the initial idea through publicity, is successful only to the extent that we connect with the one person we are trying to attract to the event. Finding a way to make our event connect with someone is not always easy.

Today, it demands that we go beyond just knowing who that person is to something deeper—understanding, respect, and empathy. Fundamentally, everyone has needs, wants, hopes, and values. Your church, auxiliary, or committee, as a unit, also has needs, wants, hopes, and values. When these fundamental pieces overlap, that is called the "sweet spot."[14]

Participants' "What's in It for Me?" (WIIFM Syndrome)

I shortened this phrase by just calling it WIIFM. Simply stated, it means people are more concerned about themselves than they are about you. They are more concerned about their issues than your issues. I tell event planners, people may like you, but they love themselves. It does not matter if the speaker at your event

---

[14] Lisa Fortini-Campbell, *Hitting the Sweet Spot* (Chicago: The Copy Workshop, a division of Bruce Bendinger Creative Communications, Inc., 2001), pp. 24-28.

is renowned as the bishop of the universe. If that wonderful speaker cannot meet a specific need, want, hope, or value, your potential participant may not attend the event.

What are some ways you have tried to attract individuals to your events? Sometimes you may have to speak with a person in private, call him or her on the phone, or stop him or her in church before he or she leaves. People like to feel valued, and talking with them directly meets that fundamental need.

Unfortunately, I have noticed that planning committees spend the least amount of time discussing what the participants *need* rather than what *they* want the event to accomplish. Yes, we want people to be saved. Yes, we want people to be encouraged, to hold on a little longer. However, to "hold"—what does that mean? What if due to the economy, people need creative ways to fix a meal for five for under ten dollars? Or how to wait on their spouse and pay tithes when all they have is just ...?

If we do not spend time understanding the basic needs of our targeted audience, the event may be nice, but not relevant. It may be moving, but not memorable.

CHAPTER 10

REVIEW THE EVENT LIFE CYCLE

"Wisdom is the principal thing; therefore get wisdom:
and with all your getting get understanding."
—Proverbs 4:7

The Event Life Cycle - *P.E.A.C.E.*

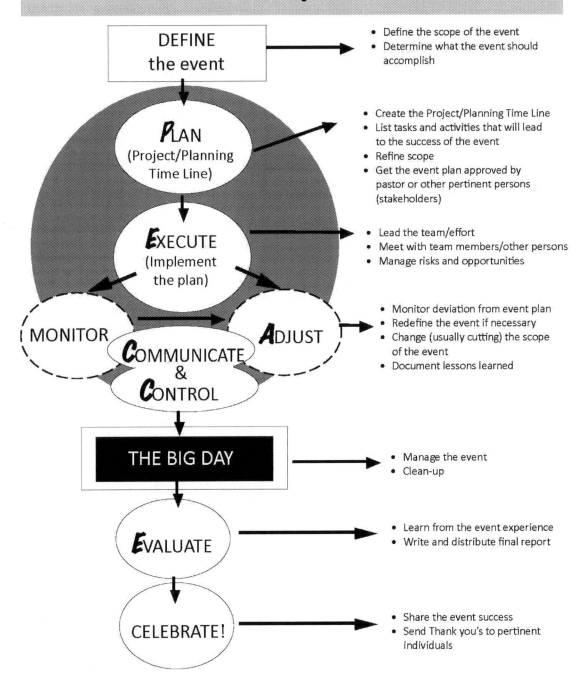

DEFINE the event
- Define the scope of the event
- Determine what the event should accomplish

PLAN (Project/Planning Time Line)
- Create the Project/Planning Time Line
- List tasks and activities that will lead to the success of the event
- Refine scope
- Get the event plan approved by pastor or other pertinent persons (stakeholders)

EXECUTE (Implement the plan)
- Lead the team/effort
- Meet with team members/other persons
- Manage risks and opportunities

MONITOR

ADJUST

COMMUNICATE & CONTROL
- Monitor deviation from event plan
- Redefine the event if necessary
- Change (usually cutting) the scope of the event
- Document lessons learned

THE BIG DAY
- Manage the event
- Clean-up

EVALUATE
- Learn from the event experience
- Write and distribute final report

CELEBRATE!
- Share the event success
- Send Thank you's to pertinent individuals

The Event Life Cycle

Every event has a beginning, middle, and end. Even if the event occurs annually, there is a time when the planning actually begins and when it ends. Although it may seem that the culminating activity is the big day, this is not necessarily accurate, as there will be things that must be addressed after the event is over to bring it to its actual conclusion.

The event life cycle has five phases. Using the acronym P.E.A.C.E., each phase has a specific charge. If all five phases are executed successfully, the process will produce a well-planned, organized, and thought-through event. Since the events we plan are for the God of all peace, the planning, if guided by His Spirit, should be peaceful as well.

Events provide one way to help us accomplish God's will through offering activities that edify the body of Christ, strengthen the brethren, and ultimately save souls. Our challenge becomes understanding *how* He wants us to accomplish this in the how-tos and whose responsibility in each of those areas. Knowing the difference between the voice of God, our own voice, and the Devil's deceitful voice is critically important when doing the work of the Lord. Admittedly, there have been times that I totally missed the mark, believing I was getting direction from God, only to learn later that it was not Him and my hard work and efforts turned out to be a complete mess. In retrospect, I appreciate the experience I gained in those early years that has helped me to learn how to wait on God rather than jump into something without His direction.

Throughout the rest of the book, we will use the P.E.A.C.E. systematic approach to planning our event. The P.E.A.C.E. system will guide us through the complex tasks associated with organizing the event. It is our blueprint, a plan that includes the overall vision of the event, with particular attention given to the details.

- A blueprint is a foundation—something you use to accomplish a task.
- More generally, the term *blueprint* has come to be used to refer to any detailed plan.
- The blueprint provides both an overview and details of the project.
- It is a tool to make sure you cross every "T" and dot every "I."
- Types of blueprints you may be familiar with include

- marketing blueprints,
- building/construction blueprints,
- financial blueprints, and
- business plan blueprints.

So, why not create a blueprint for event planning?

The forms in this chapter are provided online at *lynneshivers.com* website.

Whether you are new to the event profession or a seasoned planner, the following information will assist you in the event-planning process. The work that lies before you cannot be taken casually. With the myriad of tasks associated with event planning, using this system will enable you to simplify tasks and make you a more confident coordinator. These steps can be modified based on the specific needs of the event. Although we will be able to cut, remove, change, or alter any part of a particular task, we will have to remember that changing one aspect will cause a domino effect to a specific task in another functional area.

The P.E.A.C.E. framework places you in the driver's seat and instructs you how to define the event's purpose, create the planning time line, schedule meetings and assign tasks, select and motivate team members, evaluate long-term results, develop the budget, and monitor the planning of the event. As people tend to gravitate toward doing things they love, you may find that there may be certain aspects of the planning you will enjoy the most. On the other hand, you may also learn that if there are certain things you dislike, you may be inclined to be overly concerned about that aspect of the event just to be sure it is addressed properly. Let's say, for example, that you detest standing in long lines—bank, gas station, grocery store, it does not matter. If you find there are more than two people in the line ahead of you, your hands start to sweat, your nerves get rattled, and you feel a migraine coming on. In fact, it's reported that at the local grocery store, you have been banned because you would literally count the groceries in people's baskets to ensure they have the limited number of restricted items in the quick checkout aisle. Taking this into consideration, since standing in line a long time may be a pet peeve for you, why not during the planning spend time coordinating the registration and lunch lines to ensure they flow quickly and smoothly for the participants?

Define the Event

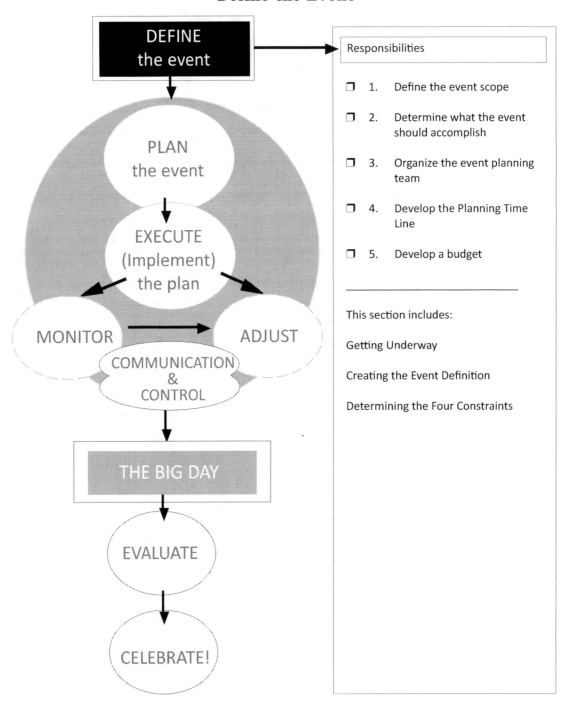

DEFINE
the event

PLAN
the event

EXECUTE
(Implement)
the plan

MONITOR

ADJUST

COMMUNICATION
&
CONTROL

THE BIG DAY

EVALUATE

CELEBRATE!

Responsibilities

☐ 1. Define the event scope

☐ 2. Determine what the event should accomplish

☐ 3. Organize the event planning team

☐ 4. Develop the Planning Time Line

☐ 5. Develop a budget

This section includes:

Getting Underway

Creating the Event Definition

Determining the Four Constraints

The most important part of any building structure is its foundation. Without a strong foundation, all other parts of a building are jeopardized. This applies also to an event. Our foundation for the event includes a good *definition*, with goals and objectives, imperatives (must-haves), and desirables (nice-to-haves) clearly written.

The event definition is a one-sentence description that includes a verb (some examples are explained in the next section). It is not a paragraph, but simply an agreed-upon short statement of the event. It contains parameters or specifics of the event. A good event definition helps you to stay focused on what you want to accomplish.

We learned from conducting a needs analysis for our women's conference that

- 58 percent of the women between the ages of thirty-two to fifty-five were concerned with juggling the demands of work, family, and life;
- 22 percent wanted an opportunity to just relax;
- 10 percent wanted the conference to be affordable;
- 7 percent wanted to know how to feel appreciated and valued; and
- 3 percent had various interests, such as entrepreneurial opportunities, marriage, and maturing in Christ.

With our needs analysis now in hand, we have a better understanding of how to plan. The planning process includes a framework for decision making that is flexible enough to be applied to smaller events of under fifty persons or conferences of thousands. Our particular conference is expecting approximately seventy-five women to attend the event at *Life Is Meaningful Community Church.*

Four Constraints

As you start the planning, you will need to think about four basic constraints that set the parameters for the event. The constraints are the walls or limits surrounding your planning. Constraints help to provide direction on what the most important thing is that needs to be met above the other three for the event to be considered a success in the eyes of the stakeholder. The constraints also tell us how much can or cannot be done. Remember, the stakeholder is the one who gives the final approval that the primary goal of the event has been met. Too often we think events have the same competing goal, but just as Jesus said there could only be one master, there can only be one main goal or driver. Although there can be subgoals, each event can have only one driver, and the planning reflects that it is the main thing.

The four constraints are

- *scope* (how small or large the event will be),
- *cost* (budget),
- *time* (when it will be held), and
- *customer satisfaction* (both the owner/client and participant).

The one constraint that steers the other three is called a *driver.* The driver shows where the resources will be directed in order for the event to happen. For example, if you are working with a limited *budget,* you may have to eliminate some perks to make the nice-to-haves not take you out of the budget. What if the driver were *time*? Let's say you got started late with the planning, so resources, such as finding additional helpers or adjusting the scope may have to be applied to ensure the event occurs at the scheduled time. Time can also pertain to how much actual time is given to make the event happen.

Hindsight Does Not Have to Be 20-20

Understanding the Driver

Your pastor wants to have a fund-raiser that will bring in enough revenue to cover the costs of another, larger event later in the year. The idea that went forth was a concert with the home choir. However, as things ensued, the planning committee believed that to bring in revenue, a local celebrity should be invited. The day of the event, yes, the artist did bring in a crowd, but his

---

entertainment fee, as well as per diem costs for his background singers and musicians, actually yielded very little revenue. In the end, the driver of the event—sizable revenue—was not met. A familiar saying goes, "Hindsight is 20-20." However, I believe that in this instance, if the driver were kept in the front of everyone's mind, doing anything that took away from—rather than added to—the goal would not have been considered.

Our first attempt at defining the event reads:

Plan a conference for approximately seventy-five women on balancing work, life, and family issues to be held on Saturday, August 14, 2010, at a cost of $55 per person.

This is a simple definition but works because it contains three specific constraints:

1. *Scope*—"Conference for seventy-five women on balancing work, life, and family" (this explains how many are expected, which helps the cost to be justified or shows how it will need to be justified if altered later, if necessary).
2. *Time*—August 14 (lets us know when).
3. *Cost*—$55 per person. The amount should cover everything (registration materials, meals, rental items, speaker honoraria or gifts).

So, you may be wondering if location should be added. It certainly can; however, I suggest leaving the location for a separate discussion, as it may impact the overall cost if the event were moved to a public meeting facility (such as a hotel or conference center). If location is important and you want it included in the event definition, it can be added this way:

Plan a conference at Life Is Meaningful Community Church *for approximately seventy-five women on balancing work, life, and family issues to be held on Saturday, August 14, 2010, at a cost of $55 per person.*

Another constraint we can include is *customer satisfaction*. Sometimes you may want to include a satisfaction component because of previous experiences.

For our example, let's say in our study of previous conference evaluations, people expressed some level of boredom. Additionally, at the post-briefing meeting, the pastor was concerned that it went over budget.

To include these items into the definition, we could say:

Plan a relaxing and exciting *conference for approximately seventy-five women on balancing work, life, and family issues to be held on Saturday, August 14, 2010, that* does not exceed *$55 per person.*

Or just for fun, let's add all the constraints in our definition: *Plan a relaxing and exciting conference for approximately seventy-five women on issues such as balancing work, life, and family on Saturday, August 14, 2010, not to exceed $55 per person.*

Must-Haves and Nice-to-Haves

Since we have an agreed-upon event definition, we need to address what participants have expressed as *must-haves* and *nice-to-haves*. The must-haves are the basic minimums that have to be included in order for the conference to be considered a success. They are what people are expecting. The must-haves can also be things that you believe are important to the success of the event. The nice-to-haves are things that would really set the conference apart. They are the *wow* factor. However, there can be items on the nice-to-have list that can get moved to the must-have column. For example, at a conference I planned on my secular job, a nice-to-have item was to give each participant a passport with his or her photo in it. In time this became an essential goal and the task was moved to the must-have column. Quite a task, as there were more than four hundred participants! We did accomplish this goal, and it was a big hit at the conference and created the *wow* factor we wanted when people arrived and picked up their registration materials.

With an event definition, must-haves, and nice-to-haves in hand (see example on the next page), our conference foundation is beginning to develop.

EVENT DEFINITION

Reminder: the Event Definition is a one sentence description of the event. This task should be done as a team and agreed upon by all members and major stakeholders of what the end result will be. Include in the definition the end result of the event, completion date (time) and budget.

Plan a relaxing and exciting one day conference for approximately 75 women on issues such as balancing work, life, and family issues on Saturday, August 14, 2010, not to exceed $55 per person.

End-results objective - List the imperatives (must haves) and the desirables (nice to have).

Imperatives Event must-have these things in order to be a success:	**Desirables** We can add these additional things to meet the stakeholders nice-to-have list:

Must-Haves	Nice-to-Haves
1. Have topics that deal with juggling work, life and family	1. Invite massage therapy students to offer massages
2. Create opportunity for networking and fellowship (getting-to-know-you activities)	2. Address issues related to starting your own business
3. Have topics that deal with insecurity and low self-esteem	3. Workshop on defining your fashion style
4. Have workshops on developing a closer walk with Jesus	

CHAPTER 11

DEVELOP THE P.E.A.C.E. SYSTEM

P—pray and project planning time line

E—execute the plan

A—adjust where necessary

C—communicate and control the plan

E—evaluate

Pray and Project Planning Time Line

"P"

The pray and project planning time line is the most important part of the planning process for the event and is the longest part of the P.E.A.C.E. system. It is your blueprint. It contains the tasks that will be performed in each of the major function areas. As the event coordinator, you will use the blueprint to write down the tasks and monitor all activities that are to be executed by individuals or committees. The time line includes each task that is to be done, who is responsible for performing the task, a start date and end date for each task, the completion percentage, and notes.

The time line is similar to a space launch and indicates the countdown of the work to be done. Tasks begin with the number ten (10) and proceed consecutively to zero (0). Tasks assigned to 10 are to be done at the very beginning of the process, and zero is assigned to activities on the day of the event. As much as possible try to create the length of time between 10 and 0 in fairly equal intervals. Tasks are assigned numbers depending on when they should occur along the continuum.

For example, in a twelve-month planning cycle, five represents the halfway point. The sixth month and tasks that should occur then will be assigned the number 5. The designations +1, +2, and so on indicate priorities for tasks to be done after the event.

P.E.A.C.E.ful Event Planning
Blank Time Line

Use this countdown as a model to list the tasks as they should be ranked sequentially in the planning process. Where 5 is the mid-point, everything above that should be done.		
PROJECT/PLANNING TIME LINE	**COUNTDOWN**	**Assigned To/Notes**
Conceptualize scope of event	10	
Develop Budget	10	
Review scope of event w/pastor/client/stakeholders	10	
Get approval for scope, plan and budget	9	
Contact venue's scheduling office	9	
Review information on site(s)	9	
Visit venue/facility site(s)	9	
Review options for promoting event	9	
Submit key questions and procedures to planning committee	9	
Establish an account	9	
Develop first draft of program design	8	
Review draft design	8	
Select facility	8	
Negotiate details with facility coordinator	8	
Confirm arrangements with facility in writing	8	
Outline promotional plan	8	
Review plan with others/supervisors	8	
Review budget plan with others/supervisors	8	
Determine preregistration information	8	
Make floor plan	8	
Develop evaluation instrument in final form	8	
Critique evaluation instrument	8	
Revise first draft of program design	7	
Select keynote and workshop speakers	7	
Prepare room-needs request form	7	
Finalize promotional plan	7	
Identify registration procedures	7	
Prepare sample registration form	7	
Contact suggested workshop speakers	7	
Send confirmation letter to selected workshop speakers (first letter)	6	
Include room-needs checklist in program committee's letter	6	
Process preregistration applications	6	
Assign space as appropriate	6	
Order supplies and equipment	6	
Check AV/lunch feedback from workshop speakers	6	
Follow up where needed	5	
Prepare program	5	

P.E.A.C.E.ful Event Planning
Blank Time Line

Serve as liaison to printer	5	
Identify on-site registration needs	5	
Reserve use of AV equipment	5	
Confirm site arrangements with facility in writing	4	
Confirm lodging for speakers	4	
Arrange special transportation	4	
Determine site food and beverage needs; confirm arrangements	4	
Coordinate registration setup	4	
Coordinate printing of final program with printers	4	
Obtain list of area restaurants	4	
Arrange for preparation of necessary signs	3	
Arrange for staff at registration/sign-in	3	
Prepare letter of welcome for workshop speakers (if applicable)	3	
Arrange transportation for workshop speakers	2	
Review list of participants	2	
Arrange for receipt of monies at site	2	
Check on supplies	2	
Confirm final site arrangements	1	
Final contact with all pertinent parties	1	
Supervise delivery of equipment, supplies and program books	1	
Prepare registration/on-site lists	1	
Prepare important instructions for staff	1	
Check last-minute registration needs	1	
Check on status of bills	1	
DAY OF EVENT		
Inspect session rooms	0	
Monitor transportation arrangements	0	
Distribute and collect evaluations	0	
FOLLOWING EVENT		
Review evaluation results	+1	
Send thank-you letters to speakers	+1	
Review bills	+1	
Ensure return of supplies and equipment	+1	
Tabulate evaluation results	+1	
Arrange for closing account	+1	
Prepare and final reports and distribute to pastor/client/stakeholders	+2	
Review "lessons learned" and file in binder or folder for next year/event	+3	

Keep the Devil out. Trying to get a handle on a complex job is virtually impossible unless some way is found to conceptualize it. Studies have shown that the human mind is able to deal only with little bits of information at one time. Feeling overwhelmed can easily be reached very quickly for even small events. To reduce the complexity, the tool of choice is the project/planning time line.

CHAPTER 12

EXECUTE THE PLAN

"E"

"Whatever you do, work at it with all your heart,
as working for the Lord, not for men."
—Colossians 3:23

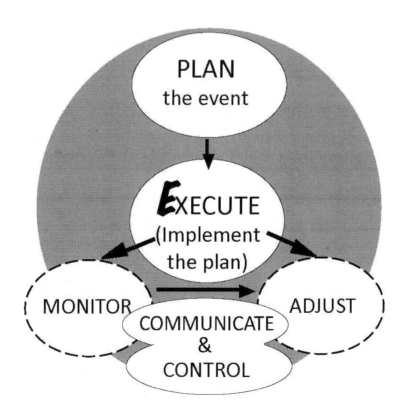

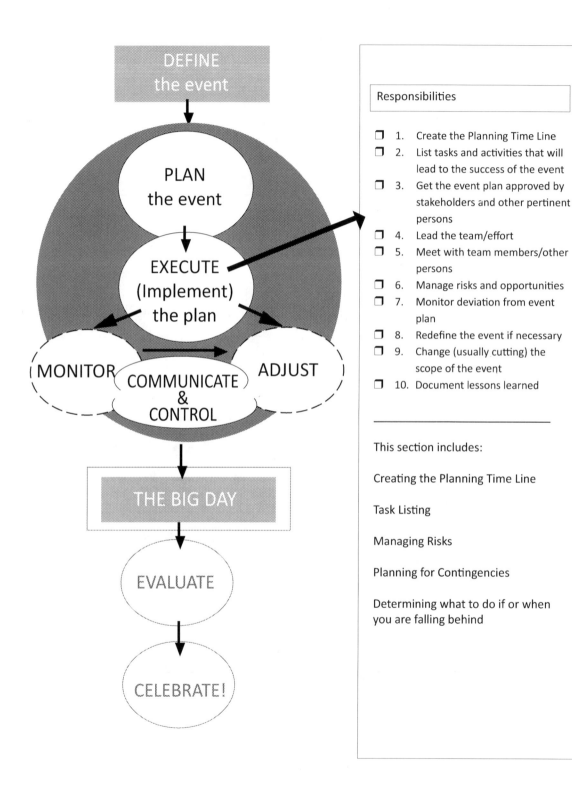

DEFINE
the event

PLAN
the event

EXECUTE
(Implement)
the plan

MONITOR

COMMUNICATE
&
CONTROL

ADJUST

THE BIG DAY

EVALUATE

CELEBRATE!

Responsibilities

☐ 1. Create the Planning Time Line
☐ 2. List tasks and activities that will lead to the success of the event
☐ 3. Get the event plan approved by stakeholders and other pertinent persons
☐ 4. Lead the team/effort
☐ 5. Meet with team members/other persons
☐ 6. Manage risks and opportunities
☐ 7. Monitor deviation from event plan
☐ 8. Redefine the event if necessary
☐ 9. Change (usually cutting) the scope of the event
☐ 10. Document lessons learned

This section includes:

Creating the Planning Time Line

Task Listing

Managing Risks

Planning for Contingencies

Determining what to do if or when you are falling behind

Work the Plan

After you have created the project/task planning time line, start executing or implementing the plan. The time line will make sure you stay on track with where you are in the planning process.

Your job is that of manager, motivator, and arbitrator. Keep in touch with key planning people, such as the pastor or the director of the program. If you are working with a team of people, ask them to report to you at designated intervals. (Mark those on the planning time line with a percentage if that work has been done. Keep changing the percentages as you get updates until the task is completed, which is 100 percent.)

In addition, you need to keep each person informed of the progress, changes, and problems of the other committee members. Encourage your team members to report problems when they need help. Of course, the speed of your response will be determined by your ability to anticipate potential problems. When planning covers many months, expect personnel changes as a result of job transfers, illnesses, and the like. As the event planner, you should be prepared to fill vacancies when they occur.

The first page of the planning time line provides an overview of the conference and provides at a glance the details: the goals (purpose), budget, targeted audience, and so on. It also highlights the planning deliverables, which are the major tasks that need to be accomplished. Subsequent pages are the individual tasks and who is assigned to accomplish that task.

Women's Conference	
Planning Time Line	
Conference Date: August 14, 2010	
Sponsored by: Life is Meaningful Community Church	
Theme: "Taking It All in Balance"	
Purpose of Conference	Plan a relaxing and exciting one day conference for approximately seventy-five women on issues such as balancing work, life, and family.
Project Lead and Core Planning Team	Katie Elam (KE), Mark Irish (MI), Kim Stanford (KS), Paula Thompson (PT), Darlene Randolf-Jackson (DRJ), Robin Samson (RS), Marilyn Weber (MW) and Denise Hanson (DH)
Email Group Name	WomensConference2010@yahoo.com
Event Manager	Lynne Shivers (LS)
Reoccurring Theme/s	• Fellowship • Socializing • Prayers
Targeted Audience	Women at LIMC and surrounding community (approx. 285)
Expected Attendance	75-100 during day and excess of 200 for evening services
Budget	$4,500
Registration Fee	$55.00 per person

Yearly Deliverables	• Schedule conference for mid-May	Completed 6/10/09
	• Select facility and secure all rooms needed	Completed 6/10/09
	• Select core planning team	Completed
	• Select meeting dates and times convenient for planning committee members	Completed 11/17/09
	• Assess needs and interest of audience	
	• Confirm theme is of interest and important to intended audience	Completed 2/10
	• Select keynote speaker	Completed 12/17/09
	• Select workshops and massages	Completed 2/25/10
	• Create reward system at conference (certificate in each participants folder)	Completed 5/18/10
	• Complete design of conference logo	Completed 3/5/10
	• Develop promotional communication materials	Completed
	• Conduct conference	Completed 5/26/10
	• Evaluate and debrief conference	Completed 6/17/10
	• Schedule next year's conference date	Completed. Next year's conference date: 8/13/11

Conference Date/Time	Sat., August 14, 2010; 8:00 am - 12:00 noon
Location	Life is Meaning Community Church, 222 Your Town, USA 23451
Keynote Speaker	Pastor Pam Sutherland, *Crossroads Church, Other Town, USA 23456*
Theme	Taking It All in Balance
Schedule	***Saturday, August 14, 2010*** 7:00-8:00AM – Prayer 8:00-8:30AM – Continental Breakfast and Registration 8:30-4:00PM – Registration

	8:45-9:45AM – Opening Remarks and Address
	10:00-11:00AM – Seminar 1
	11:10AM-12:10PM – Seminar 2
	12:10-1:00PM – Lunch
	1:00-2:00PM – Panel Discussion
	2:10-3:10PM – Seminar 3
	3:10-3:30PM – Fellowship in Grand Hall
	3:30-4:30PM- Closing program and Remarks
Breakout Sessions (workshops)	• The Me in Me Got in the Way of Us Again (f) • Getting Past the Mask to See You! (s) • How to Pray for Others and Not Get In Their Business (p)

TASK LISTING

#	TASK	Assigned to	Begin Date	End Date	%Complt	Notes
JANUARY						
1	Select date for next year's conference	LS	1/10/10	1/10/10	100%	
2	Ensure date is on pastor's calendar; send hold-the-date to LIMCC administration	, LS	1/10/10	1/10/10	100%	
3	Discuss with pastor/leader the budgeted amount for this year	DRJ	1/10/10	1/10/10	100%	
4	Select committee members	ALL	1/10/10	1/10/20	100%	
FEBRUARY						
5	First meeting with committee members: initial discussion on goals, theme, workshop topics, and speakers	All	2/16/10	2/16/10	100%	
6	Develop detailed budget	LS	2/17/10	2/17/10	100%	
7	Meet with committee; continue discussion on items in #2. Review revised timeline and budget. Discuss key issues conference must address, keynote speaker, workshops	All	2/17/10	2/17/10	100%	Christian Humorist to speak on transitions; "Humor Lady"
8	Develop catchy theme title (Balancing It All)	All	2/17/10	2/17/10	100%	
9	Return signed contract	LS	2/17/10	2/17/10	100%	
10	Reserve Board Room for Registration Folder Stuffing Day	LS	2/17/10	2/18/010	100%	
11	Get event account for billing	RS			100%	
12	Contact speaker: Pastor Pam Sutherland	LS	2/17/10	2/21/10	100%	Pastor Sutherland agreed
13						
MARCH						
14	Meet with committee: finalize keynote speaker, determine workshop titles and potential speakers, assign who will make initial contact to seminar speakers	All	3/14/10	3/14/10	100%	
15	Draft Speaker AV confirmation letter and AV Needs form	LS	Moved to April	Moved to April	100%	
16	Initial contact to workshop speakers	KE	3/10/10	3/10/10	100%	
17	Inform Sis. Lynne of speakers' consent to speak; send speaker contact information (e-mail address, etc) to her	All	3/11/10	3/12/10	100%	
18	Initial inquiry to main speaker if she consents to speak, send contact information to Sis. Lynne	LS	3/17/10	3/17/10	100%	Done as Lynne was the contact with the

Meetings, Structure, and Agendas

Meetings are very important to ensure the planning is on schedule, to answer questions or discuss issues that the whole committee should participate in, and to brainstorm. Depending on when the planning started, if you have six or more months out before the event, I suggest holding meetings

- once a month for events six months out,
- every two weeks during the three months before the event, and
- every week during the month before the event.

Unless the pastor or someone in higher authority is present, the event manager should run the meeting. Although I think at times it is important to discuss some things at length, for topics where there is not enough information and the discussion seems to be going nowhere, select a subcommittee to investigate and return an answer either via e-mail or a report at the next meeting. Your goal as the event manager is to get to all of the items on the agenda. Basically, you want to know if things are going along smoothly and if not, who is having issues so that they can be addressed. Any member having a personal issue should not be openly discussed at the meeting; just schedule a meeting to privately meet with that person.

Meetings do not have to last an entire hour just because it was scheduled that way. In addition, if there is not enough time to discuss something, consider postponing that topic until a later meeting.

Conference-Call Meetings and Online Meetings

With the availability nowadays for convenient ways to meet, do not just rely on the physical presence of your committee to get together. Consider free conference-call lines and online companies such as join.me and GoToMeeting.com. I tend to use the conference-call line when we need it, and the best time I have found is late in the evenings because of people's job schedules. The join.me and GoToMeeting are good when you need to share information for everyone to see.

Agenda

The agenda should be sent to committee members prior to the meeting. Sometimes doing so helps to remind someone who may need to report back information. Having that extra day or two, or even just a couple of hours, can provide just enough time for him or her to prepare. The agenda should begin and end with prayer.

Sample Agenda

   I. **Opening Prayer**
  II. **Scripture**
 III. **Chairman's Comments**
  IV. **Committee Reports**
   V. **Old Business**
  VI. **New Business**
 VII. **Next Steps**
VIII. **Adjournment**
  IX. **Closing Prayer**

Minutes

Taking notes of the meeting helps to remind everyone what was discussed and, most importantly, which action items need to be done before the next meeting or at some point during the planning process. If possible, circulate the minutes with the agenda before the next meeting. Basically, you want to capture action items, not the full discussion on each item.

Women's Conference Planning Meeting Minutes May 4, 2010 • 2:00 p.m. • LIMCC Main Boardroom		
Item	**Action**	**Who**
Prayer	Prayer and Scripture	Minister Phyllis Gatling
April minutes	Read minutes from April 15. Changes: a. Correct time of reception is 4:00–6:00 p.m. b. Sister Beverly Curtling is donating the water bottles, not Brother Scott.	Sister Georgina Scott
Review of budget	No corrections	Brother James Chaines
Discussion of workshop speakers	Speakers to be contacted a. (Name) b. (Name) c. (Name)	Sister Beverly Curtling
Participants' certificates	Check into cost for paper	Evangelist Michelle Tourney
Closing prayer		Evangelist Tourney

CHAPTER 13

ADJUST WHERE NECESSARY

"A"

"Man's goings are of the Lord; how can a man then understand his own way?"
—Proverbs 20:24

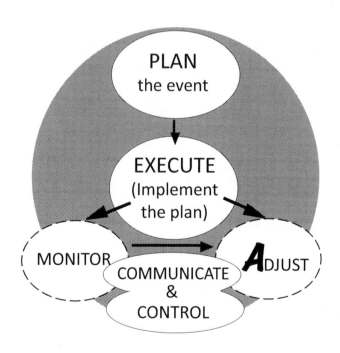

Flexibility is Important

As you are moving along in the planning, sometimes things can change that require a modification from the original idea. This happened to me one time when a large event, initially scheduled to be held at a hotel, was later moved to a church instead. The decision to move required canceling the event at the hotel, informing people who had already purchased tickets that the venue had changed, and meeting with the pastor and church key contacts on the menu, decorations, and so on.

When such a change occurs, it is not a time to get upset, for God knew the event was going to move. It is how we handle the stress at times like this that shows our character. Trust the Lord to lead you in the direction you should go and ask Him to keep your mind in a perfect way.

Monitor the Process

A good event planner understands the possibility that certain things can go wrong that will affect the planning process. To anticipate which things can put a wrench in your planning, identify major areas for the event (such as staffing, keynote/workshop speakers, food and beverage, program materials, travel, electronic needs, rentals, and so on) and have a back-up plan in place. I have learned to ask the following questions about what could go wrong.

1. What is a critical resource? What will we do if they leave?
2. Who else do we need involvement from? Are they committed to helping us achieve our goals?
3. Is there a risk of technical glitches? How will we handle them?
4. What if the materials do not arrive on time?
5. Are members of our team properly trained? If not, what do we need to do?
6. What if the keynote speaker or a workshop speaker is delayed or cannot attend the event at the last moment?

Contingency Plan

A contingency plan is a backup solution for an unexpected occurrence. It is your plan B in the event something goes wrong with the original plan. It does not mean that you have to have two speakers lined up in case one does not show. But you can always address what you should do with the stakeholder well in advance if that does happen so if something does go wrong, you can jump into action.

In addition, if possible, I would add new tasks to the project/planning time line to prevent the problem from occurring. The following chart will help you to think of backup or contingency plans.

Contingency: A possibility that must be prepared for

Task	What could go right/wrong	How/When will I know?	What could I do?
Select hotel within walking distance	Hotel completely booked	Checking availability	Investigate other hotels

For your event, use this sample to jot down contingency plans if things do not turn out the way you hope:

Task	What could go right/wrong	How/When will I know?	What could I do?

Keep the Devil out. The key to solving any problem is catching it as early as possible. Do not let the Devil convince you that ignoring an issue will make it go away. A problem caught soon enough may be trivially easy to solve. However, the same problem caught too late may be impossible to solve.

What to Do If You Start Falling Behind

The project/task planning time line can also alert you when you are falling behind in finishing tasks. One way of determining this is to visually look at the time line. As you proceed from month to month, everything from the previous month should be at 100 percent. If you see a lot of tasks that are not fully completed, that means you are starting to fall behind schedule. To get back on track, consider four options:

1. Review the incomplete tasks. Can any be eliminated? Moved to another month further in the schedule?
2. Examine future tasks and decide whether aspects can be eliminated that will not affect either the must-haves or nice-to-haves.
3. Consider offering an incentive for on-time completion of the event.
4. Consider deploying more resources, such as additional money. (For example, if you had someone who was supposed to create a publicity flier for no charge but is way behind schedule, see if you can hire someone to create it.)

Solution Strategies

Below are some strategies you can implement when things seem to not be running smoothly:

- Renegotiate—If something is not working out as planned, is there room for negotiation? For example, let's say the speaker you want is not available on Friday, when you intended to give the conference kickoff address. Is he or she available on that Saturday morning for the breakfast keynote? This may even help to get more people out at an early hour if the speaker is a draw.
- Recover during later stages—If time has gotten past you, pick up speed later when you can. However, oftentimes when you are making up for lost time, this means that more hours will have to be packed in a shorter period of time.
- Narrow event scope—This can change one of the four constraints. Sometimes we may need to cut out some things to stay within budget or time.
- Request more help—Do not be afraid or too proud to ask for help. However, if you delegate the task, the end product may not be as you would have done it. Is it okay enough to pass? Too often we want something done exactly as we would have, but you already do not have the time or energy. So be thankful for the help and let it go.
- Accept substitution—See if you can substitute something else that might be able to be there in time for your event for what you initially had in mind. One time I wanted a professionally designed item for a group of women. However, we missed the order deadline. Instead, we asked someone who had done similar work in the past to make the item for us. No, she was not a professional. But the end product was good enough ... and the women's group loved it!

CHAPTER 14

COMMUNICATION AND CONTROL

"C"

"The words of a man's mouth are as deep waters, and
the wellspring of wisdom as a flowing brook."
—Proverbs 18:4

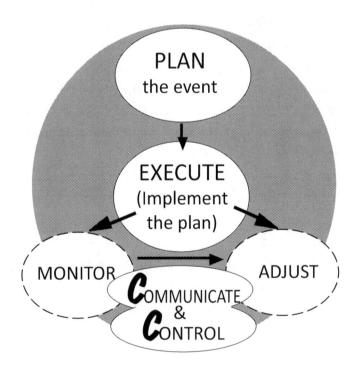

Communication Is Not an Action Plan!

Have you ever experienced this? An announcement is made about an upcoming event at the church. The announcer asks people to see the bulletin for more information and to contact him, her, or a committee member for tickets. Soon after, the committee is concerned because only a few tickets have been sold. So, more announcements are made. There is even a table set up in the lobby for people to purchase tickets. The day of the event, the numbers in attendance are low. The committee is bewildered. Much worse, the pastor is disappointed. What happened? *Communication is not an action plan.* Getting people to act—purchase a ticket, sign up to volunteer, bring baked goods to the bake sale, and so on—takes more than just *asking* them to respond. You have to generate an interest inside them to respond. You have to get them to listen, not just hear.

How Does Your Target Audience Listen?

Build it and they will come. It is a nice story line. However, churches can no longer rely solely on an *announcement of an event and the members automatically coming to the event.* People have so many other distractions that ... oh yes, now, where were we?

Every event has a "voice," a message for a group of people, the audience, to hear, experience, and appreciate. The right audience for that event will have an ear to hear what the event is trying to say to them. Your challenge is figuring out if your message will reach the right people.

Story

A few years ago, my office was reopening its building after months of a major reconstruction. Many hours of planning went into the multiday open house, which would culminate with a celebrity speaker on the final evening. The keynote speaker was an African American actress who impersonated historical figures. We anticipated an audience of about six hundred people.

Three days before the event, I received a call from the booking agent informing me that the speaker had a sore throat and was recommended by her doctor to cancel the event. I was stunned. With an anticipated audience of six hundred, what would I tell my boss? I was the event planner. I was the one who had to ensure the event would happen. After a few prayers and rebuking the Devil to ensure his head did not surface in the confusion, one plan was to tell my boss that not only was our speaker not coming, but oh well, my boss seemed like the perfect backup.

Knowing that wouldn't fly, I contacted the speakers' bureau and insisted that they help me find a backup. The only person who really wasn't a celebrity was the only name speaker available. He was the photographer at Ground Zero, who received his fifteen minutes of fame by being the only photographer allowed on the premises to take pictures of the ruins where the planes struck the Twin Towers on 9/11.

My boss approved the new speaker, but the real work began. I had to think about the audience he would attract. I did not want to surprise nor disappoint six hundred people who came to be entertained by an actress. Instead, they would see the ravishing remains of one of the most devastating and historically horrific times in our history.

The issue was more than having people in seats. I had to think: who is *his* audience? Where would I find *his* interest group? What unconventional ways could I employ to get them there? Notwithstanding, I also had to consider my current anticipated audience. How would I inform them that the speaker had changed so they could make the choice whether or not to attend?

Several strategies were implemented immediately: contact the local newspaper and place an ad about the speaker change, contact local photography clubs, work with faculty and people in the community to spread the news, send electronic notifications, and place signs on marquees and in the lobby of the building.

The end result? Approximately two hundred people attended the event. The hall where they sat looked nearly empty. But when he finished his talk, he received a standing ovation—from the audience who came to hear *him*.

What made this event successful was that we were able to attract those who wanted to *hear* him and his message.

People are drawn to an event that speaks to *them*. As we tend to become involved in those things that benefit us personally (WIIFM), we have to make sure the event is meeting some kind of interest. Just sending a flier announcing your special event does not necessarily mean that people will attend. The decision to attend or not can be based on several factors: 1) the person's relationship to the person or church sending the invitation, 2) whether the event will meet a need, want, hope, or value, 3) whether they feel obligated, 4) whether there is a permanent consequence, 5) or whether it has personal intrinsic value.

Publicity and Advertising

If you look at an advertising piece in the newspaper or a flier, think about what caught your eye. An ad's sole purpose is to get you to read it. This also applies to our church fliers and advertisements. Are the graphics boring? Too complicated? Are you missing key information? In general, ads follow a certain format that appeals to the way people naturally read and retain information. Is it big enough to catch the person's attention? Do not use a lot of words in the header. Up to five or six words is max.

The graphic below demonstrates this by showing that our mind reads left to right.

1. Eye-grabbing graphics draw the person into your ad or flier.
2. Our minds naturally begin at this point and read across to #3.
3. Here is where you want to include important text.
4. Dead zone—at the bottom and away from the mind's natural focus. Include here images, such as a logo. Pharmaceutical companies tend to put their "fine print" here.
5. The call to action—what is it you want them to do? Register now? Call this number? Go to a particular website? Here is where you get them to do something other than just read. A good ad helps your eyes to flow easily.

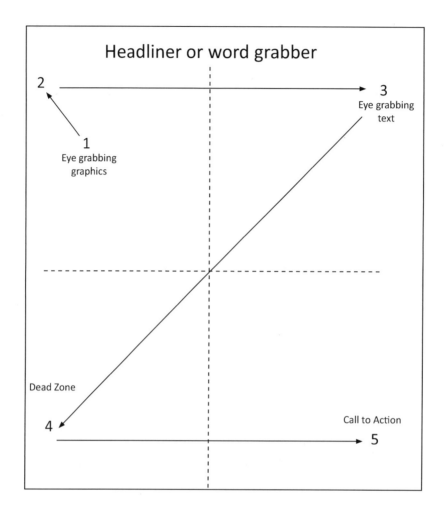

Communication about the event must be in more than just one method. You have to think about your targeted audience. As mentioned in chapter 3, there are individuals you want to attend who may comprehend information in different ways: visually, audibly, or kinesthetically. So, if you are using only one way to invite them, let's say as an announcement during service, you may be missing two-thirds of the people, who retain information differently. Similarly, if the only way people are getting information is through the church brochure or a flier, you may be missing others who won't pick up a copy.

How can you make your event announcement interesting? One group at a church was sponsoring a country-style breakfast fund-raiser. During the time announcements were being made, others simply came to the microphone to give verbal details about their upcoming events. However, her group came out in full garb! Members wore costumes made like oranges, bacon, eggs, and waffles. That certainly piqued the interest of the audience! It was unexpected. It was funny. But most of all, it was memorable. She had more than a hundred people attend the event.

Information about the upcoming event does not have to be boring! Make the graphics interesting for your intended audience. Look at the design elements. Does it appeal to that specific group? Do they "see" themselves in the graphics?

Print Materials and Mailing Schedule

Brochures

A brochure's purpose is to communicate, in an appealing format, enough information about the upcoming event to interest a potential participant. It can be mailed or personally distributed. While the youth generation today lives on electronic devices and the Internet and you can send them information by e-mail or electronic invite, the elderly generation may still prefer the personal invitation, indicating to them you cared enough to invite them personally.

The brochure should be sent well enough in advance to allow potential participants time to make their decision and to complete the necessary steps to register. When to send it will also depend on whether or not a teaser letter or flier precedes the brochure.

A general guideline for when information should be sent follows:

- If save-the-date (a teaser) precedes the brochure, then
    o send the save-the-date eight to twelve months in advance.
    o send the brochure one to three months in advance.
- If there is no advance publicity, then
    o send the brochure two to three months in advance.

Remember that preparation of the brochure can take up to two months depending on the amount of graphics work to be done, the length of time the printer needs, and who prepares the brochures for mailing.

Content

The following information is usually included in your publicity materials. Remember to include essential information, which means you have to first obtain or decide on the following:

- Objectives of events: What are the general goals and specific objectives for the planned event?
- Target population: Who might attend? What do you know about them?
- Time: How much time is available for the program?
- Budget: How much money is available for the program?
- Date(s) and times
- Location
- Description of each session
- Seminar leaders' names, titles, and affiliations
- Facility information
- Fees (clarify what they include)
- Registration form and information
- Lodging information
- Child-care arrangements
- Special events

Social Networks Work— But Don't Forget the Personal Touch

It is amazing how in such a few short years, many churches now have a presence on Facebook. Certainly, having a Facebook page is an essential step in getting people to know who you are, but not keeping it current can cause it to become old news very quickly. A recent online article on social networking reports, "Congregations that have not yet created a presence on Facebook need to do so, especially in light of recent research that shows the majority of Americans age 12 and older now have Facebook accounts."[15]

---

[15] E. S. Anderson, "Your Church's Facebook Page." *http://sowhatfaith.com/2011/06/15/your-churchs-facebook-page/* (June 15, 2011).

No matter how fast and convenient social networking may be, people still need the personal touch. An invitation sent to the house, a phone call, or other personal method can be the difference between someone attending your event or just letting the announcement go in one ear and out the other. In addition to popular social media sites such as Facebook, Twitter and Instagram, there are hundred others available at your fingertips to help promote your event. Use your imagination to think about creative ways to grab your audience's attention. Consider making a short video clip that provides a teaser of what will come or create incentives such as word games of things they will learn at the event. These are just a couple ways to get people thinking about the event well before the day. Search the web for more creative ideas.

Getting the Event on Their Mind

"Out of sight, out of mind" is a good adage to use when it comes to getting the event on the participants' mind. Most likely, if people are not thinking about your event, there is a good chance they may not attend. I like to pose this to you in this way—remember that vacation you were planning in chapter 4? Let's say you are scheduled to go on that vacation in June with a couple of good friends. Although it is only February, you are already thinking about being on the beach, a tall cold beverage in your left hand. You feel the water washing onto your toes, the soft wind blowing off the ocean. Your beach time is months away, but you have already investigated the best beaches to go to, you have already booked your room, and you have already looked at airfares. Yes, you have already seen yourself on the beach ... it just has not happened yet.

Just as you visualize being on that beach months away, you are making plans now to make it a reality. What people think about, they work toward. This also applies to your event. Are people thinking about being at your event? Have they blocked off that time on their calendar? Are they asking questions about the schedule? Who are the speakers? If no one has inquired about any aspect of the event, it might be a warning sign that people are not planning to attend. Employ the stategies above to get your event on their mind.

Controlling the Plan: **Planning Time Line Task List**

The planning time line's most functional feature is its task list, which helps to keep you on track with what needs to be done and who on your team has the responsibility for completing that task. It is also a tool during meetings to ensure everyone is pulling his or her load.

TASK LIST					
TASK	**Assigned to**	**Begin Date**	**End Date**	**%Complt**	**Notes**
JANUARY					
Conceptualize scope for conference: how big/small, planning time line, etc.	LS	1/10/10	1/10/10	100%	
Ensure date is on pastor's calendar; send hold-the-date to LIMCC administration.	LS	1/10/10	1/10/10	100%	
Review budget, scope of event; get expectations of stakeholders.	LS	1/10/10	1/10/10	100%	
Select committee members.	LS and Pastor	1/10/10	1/10/10	100%	

Use these guidelines to fill in the columns:

- Task—a general-enough description of the work to be done, which should fit in the space, yet be specific enough to be self-explanatory
- Assigned to—initials of the person in charge, or if the entire group, use "All"
- Begin Date—when the person or group says he/she/they can begin that task
- End Date—the projected date to conclude or finish that task
- %Complt—percent of the task that has been finished. Anything less than 100 percent should be revisted at each meeting until it is completed. Each meeting should be a move toward 100 percent completion of all tasks.
- Notes

CHAPTER 15

EVALUATION

"E"

"For God shall bring every work into judgment, with every
secret thing, whether it be good, or whether it be evil."
—Ecclesiastes 12:14

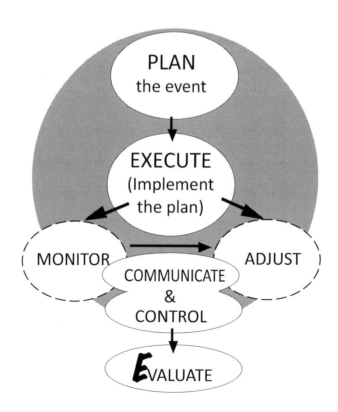

Evaluation Starts at the Beginning

Most organizations wait until after the event is over to ask participants to evaluate the event. Evaluation is *not* a post-event activity! We need to be prayerful along the way; pray with your team members and ensure the Lord is in every aspect of the planning process. If the event is to be successful, discerning whether God is in control or if the Enemy has raised his ugly head must be a continual process that starts when the planning does. If you feel something has changed in the way people are interacting with one another, if members have stopped attending meetings regularly, or if you begin to hear disillusionment and dissatisfaction with the planning process, that is cause to stop, pray, and seek God's direction in order to get back on track.

Continual evaluation notifies team members and communicates that their performance is important. The distance between what is and what should be indicates what additional resources are needed or what changes will need to be made. People will not feel offended if they think you care about them and just want to make sure they are meeting the objectives of what is expected of them.

Getting Feedback

Why is feedback important? Hearing whether the event met participants' expectations is important for three primary reasons: 1) It provides valuable information that can be used for future events, 2) you can use quotes from actual participants for future events, and 3) it informs speakers how they were received.

The most common way to get participants' feedback is through paper or electronic questionnaires. In addition to closed-ended questions that require either a yes or no answer, incoporate open-ended questions that will cause someone to share a more in-depth answer. You can also create questions that use a numeric scale, such as 1 to 5 or words like poor/fair/good/excellent.

Example of how the questions would be used in an evaluation:

1. Did the conference meet your expectations? ___Yes ___No *(closed-ended)*
2. What are ways we can improve for next year's event? *(open-ended)*

3. How well did the keynote speaker address the topic? (1—not at all to 5—excellent) *(scale)*

Debriefing with the Planning Committee

At some point, shortly after the conference, meet with the planning commmittee to debrief the event and discuss lessons learned. I typically schedule the meeting within a month of the conference. By doing so, this provides some space between the event and the meeting to allow time for objective analysis. Committee members should be directed to talk about what went well first, before jumping into what went wrong or how they would improve something for the next time. I find this process helps members to think positively about the work that went into the planning before tearing it to shreds!

Once you have discussed what went well and areas of improvement, keep the list in an electronic or paper file. Then, when the planning for the next year's event begins, pull the list out and review it early in the process. Although we may think a particular item would never be forgotten, it is amazing how a few short months (okay, for me, a few days) pass, and the never-will-forget-item becomes a *"What was it?"*

Keep the Devil out. During the debriefing session, the Enemy may use that time as another opportunity to create disorder and division among the group. I am very mindful that people tend to jump to criticizing aspects of the event rather than focusing on the positive. Start the meeting with prayer and calling for God's direction and presence. Do not let the Devil make you focus on the negative. There is so much to be thankful for; jot it down. Look it at. Then celebrate your accomplishments.

PART 5

THE BIG DAY

"It is of the Lord's mercies that we are not consumed, because his compassions
fail not. They are new every morning: great is thy faithfulness."
—Lamentations 3:22–23

Dear Lord,

This is the day the Lord has made; I will rejoice and be glad in it. I will bless the Lord at all times. Your praise shall continually be in my mouth! Lord, I ask that You go before me this day. Let Your will be done in all things. Help me to be alert. Help me to be wise in all my decisions. I pray that Your spirit permeates this event and that in everything we do, You will be pleased. Let no one get hurt. Protect us from the Enemy. Lead us not into temptation, but deliver us from evil. Help us to keep You in the frontlets of our mind. Be our strength, our guide. We bless Your name forever.

Amen.

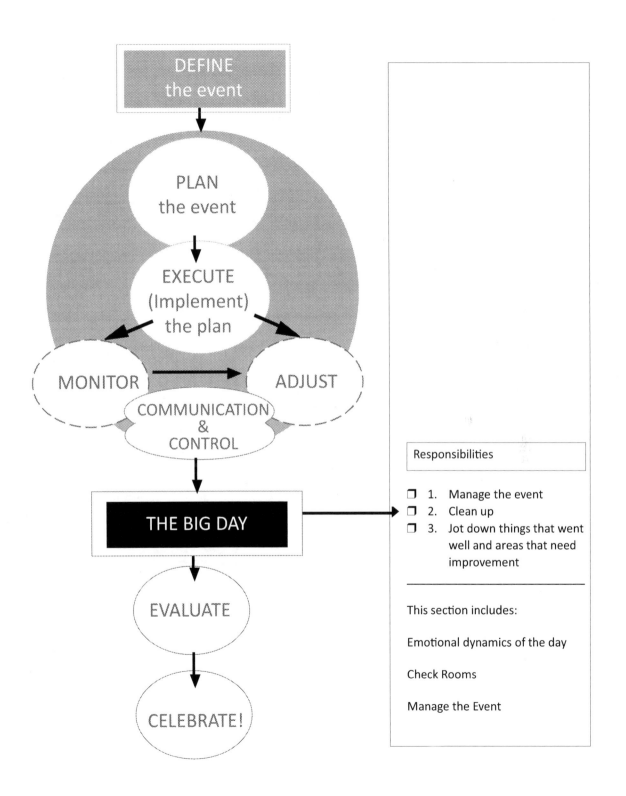

CHAPTER 16

THE BIG DAY

"For I the Lord thy God will hold thy right hand,
saying unto thee, Fear not; I will help thee."
—Isaiah 41:13

Unique Dynamics of the Event Day

This is it. You have prayed about this day. Planned for this day. Worked with others to make this day special. And now it is here. So is the Enemy. We cannot be unwise about the devices of the Devil. He does not stop at the time the event begins. No, he will try to infiltrate the entire program. Being prayerful is so very important. As the event manager, watch people's attitudes. People act happy when they are happy. Likewise they act unseemingly when they are not.

You may have to address certain attitudes on the spot. Do not see this as Sister So-and-So acting her regularly bad way. No, the Enemy is at full swing in the camp, and we have to attack him with prayer, rebuke, and restoration. You have to remember that God is in control at all times.

When you speak to a person who may be out of line, do it in love. If possible, ask the person to walk with you to a place out of the line of sight of the participants. Hear his or her side first. Do not jump in thinking that the other person told the entire story. Remember, there are his side, her side, and the truth.

Emotional Side of the Event Day

Yes, again I say, this is it! Your big day. You've dreamed about this day, you've worked hard for the past weeks or months, and now you get a chance to see it unfold before your eyes. However, there are also certain unique dynamics of the big day that are different than any other day, including the day before or the day after the event. There are particular elements that come together on that one day that will make you wonder what is in the air. I have seen typically calm and upbeat people suddenly appear as if they have been possessed by demons and become argumentative, cranky, and unyielding—just on one day, *that* day. There are things in the air that seem to only surface on that day.

What I have learned is that the more you feel out of control, the more you will act out of control.

Common Emotions That Surface:

- edginess
- crankiness
- distress
- frustration

Strategies:

- ☐ Get ample rest/sleep the day before.
- ☐ Do not change your morning routine too much.
- ☐ Give yourself ample time to get to the event location.
- ☐ Resist the temptation to make huge last-minute changes.

If you find yourself on the edge, use this word to let people know the moment you need a second to get yourself together before you can respond. Say, "H.A.L.T.," which means: "I cannot respond appropriately right now because I am either hungry, angry, lonely, or tired." Step back. Take a few moments, pray, seek God's peace, and then return to that person with an answer. You do not want to say or do something that will cause someone to see you act in an unchristian manner

(1 Cor. 13:5). It only takes one mistimed or inappropriate comment to ruin a good reputation or a good name.

Conduct a Room Spot Check

On the day of the event, a quick spot check should be made of each function room and the registration/sign-in area to be used. You may want someone to join you. Things to consider are:

- Is the room set up as you requested?
- Is all necessary equipment in the room and ready for use?
- Are all supplies in their proper places?
- Are the printed materials there and in their proper places?
- Are the signs in the correct locations?
- Do the lights work properly?
- Is the heating/cooling system functioning properly?
- Are glasses and water available in the room?

Manage the Event

Be observant and make sure things are running smoothly. Pay special attention to the following:

- Keep track of first reactions (ask staff and volunteers how they think things are going).
- Did someone wake up on the wrong side of the bed? Does anyone appear to be under a lot of stress? Pay attention to mood swings and unusual temperaments throughout the day.
- Keep a clipboard handy. On it have the schedule, plain pieces of paper to jot down notes, a pen, and the keynote speakers' bios (in case the person who is to introduce the speaker leaves his or her copy back at the office).
- Keep a positive attitude yourself.

- Wear comfortable clothing and shoes.
- Don't wear tennis shoes at professional event. Dress appropriately for the event.
- Bring an extra pair of stockings or knee-highs.
- If you have a tendency to sweat heavily, bring antiperspirant/deodorant with you (can keep your emergency supply box stored under the registration table).
- Bring mints or mouth spray, just in case.

Scriptures

"The horse is prepared against the day of battle: but safety is of the Lord" (Prov. 21:31).

"He that hath no rule over his own spirit is like a city that is broken down, and without walls" (Prov. 25:28).

PART 6

CREATIVITY PRODUCES EXCITEMENT

"Remember not the former things, neither consider the things of old."
—Isaiah 43:18

Dear Lord,

Help me in the planning of this event to manage it according to Your will. I accept the fact that without You I can do nothing. These are Your people. You know their concerns, their desires, their hopes, and their plans. Help me to seek help when needed. To find resources where I did not know there were any. To find people who want to help me. Please place in their hearts a willingness to support Your program, Your event. Help me, Lord, to plan an event that will be long remembered. Help me to be as creative as You are. No two things You have made are exactly the same!

I need You, Lord, every day. Guide my mind, my thoughts, and my hands. Let whatever I put my hands prosper. Let not the root of pride be planted in my spirit. Let not the Enemy find any place in the planning. Let all of his plans be destroyed. I give You all the glory for what You are going to do. You are my present help in the time of need. I bless Your name.

Amen.

CHAPTER 17

AN OLD THING A NEW WAY

"Be careful for nothing; but in every thing by prayer and supplication
with thanksgiving let your requests be made known unto God."
—Philippians 4:6

Keep Ideas Fresh

One of the many challenges for us as event planners is coming up with great
ideas event after event. Creativity comes from using a lot of ideas, not just one! So
research, research, research! Drew Allen Miller, in his book *Maverick Marketing ...
on a shoestring budget!,* states,

> The appropriate way to create original works is to become familiar with
> a lot of other people's ideas. Creativity is when someone takes a whole
> lot of ideas ... and uses them for inspiration. They mix, modify, swipe,
> swap, adopt and adapt until they create something truly different from
> the examples they started with. Creativity is best defined as looking
> at one thing and seeing another. Ideas are nothing more than a new
> or different arrangement of known, existing elements.[16]

Successful event planning includes both physical activity and mental cognition.
Physical activity includes things such as the actual work: writing down all relevant

---

[16] D. A. Miller, *Maverick Marketing ... on a shoestring budget!* (Kansas City, MO: Board Report
Publishing Co., Inc., 2004) p 5.

tasks and following through on them. However, most people do not realize that the second part of planning, creating mental space to think through difficult questions, work out problems, and allow concealed ideas to come to the surface, is just as important and not hard to achieve. The cognitive side of event planning flows during quiet time. Away from the hustle and bustle of life, away from internal and external noise, ideas and solutions flow.

Keep Asking "What If?"

The nice-to-haves (from chapter 10) are where you can really brainstorm for memorable *wow* factors! However, to get those great ideas brewing, try brainstorming. I heard one time that a great definition for *brainstorm* is a "brief psychological disturbance." I am not much for brainstorming, because my personality type likes to choose between two options and run with the best idea. However, I have learned that although it is a process I may not necessarily be comfortable with, the more ideas we have the better. It is a process that creative thinkers love and those without that aptitude wish they could avoid.

Drew Miller, in his book *Maverick Marketing...,* suggests asking yourself or the committee to generate some what-if ideas to make your event interesting or memorable in ways you have not thought of! Can any of these work for you?

Idea Triggers

(Insert "What If We" in Front of Each Phrase Below)

- cosponsor with another auxiliary or committee?
- find new users?
- hold it off the church site?
- target a different group?
- make it bigger or smaller?
- take stuff away from it?

Incorporating any of these new dynamics will influence the end result. Don't be afraid to try something new. Remember, "God has not given us the spirit of fear, but of power, love and a sound mind" (Tim. 1:7).

To creatively think about our women's conference, how would we ask the *what-ifs?*

- *What if* we held the event at another time of the year?
- *What if* we cosponsored it with another group/auxiliary to combine resources?
- *What if* the event were held biannually, rather than annually?
- *What if* we held it only one day instead of two?
- *What if* it were held at a conference or retreat center?

Finding the Quiet

Even Jesus spent time *alone* in prayer. He stole away to find the quiet in order to regroup, think about what was coming ahead, and talk with God. Nothing else compared to His time alone. While communicating with God, He was also consoled by God. Jesus set the example for us concerning the importance of quiet time. He took time to connect with the Father regularly, as we see in several references:

- "Then Jesus went with his disciples to a place called Gethsemane, and he said to them, 'Sit here while I go over there and pray'" (Matt. 26:36 NIV).
- "Very early in the morning, while it was still dark, Jesus got up, left the house and went off to a solitary place, where he prayed" (Mark 1:35 NIV).
- "But Jesus often withdrew to lonely places and prayed" (Luke 5:16 NIV).

When we are in a quiet time, God can speak to us, and we can hear Him. For some people, the idea of purposely taking time away from "actual" work to do "thinking stuff" is unproductive. However, it is critical to the event's success. Too often, as event planners, we shoot-fire-aim, rather than aim-fire-shoot. Quiet time creates a pause, a breather from the "noise" of the planning to answer complex questions.

What is the noise we are trying to get away from? Simply defined, "*noise* is any unwanted sound."[17] High noise levels can block, distort, change, or interfere with the meaning of a message. The Devil uses all sorts of noise in our lives to disrupt the transmission from heaven. Two types of noises are internal noises, which are our thoughts, which can be distress, anxiety, and health concerns. External noises are sounds of people talking, or annoying sounds such as chalk screeching on a blackboard or a dripping faucet.

When looking for the quiet, do not confuse it with silence. Quiet is the absence of noise or bustle. Silence, on the other hand, is the total lack of sound or noise; no sound whatsoever can be unnerving. When a hunter in the woods hears no sound from anything—animals, birds, or insects—it may indicate something is wrong. While it can appear to be difficult to find quiet at home or work, it is there. Quiet is all around us; it is just recognizing when it is present that is the challenge.

My quiet time is when I first awake. Before swinging my legs off the side of the bed, I purposefully lie there. It's quiet, although I hear the sounds of the birds giving God their morning praise. I hear cars passing by my house. And a school bus has stopped across the street to board children. I hear a siren, and my mind begins to wonder what is happening. *No, back to my quiet.* I force my thoughts away from the sirens.

In returning to my quiet, I now hear the breathing of my husband, which is deep and long; each breath tells me he's not ready for his alarm … *There were some things I needed to tell him about the cars* … *No, back to my quiet time.* It's easy to start thinking about other things, but this quiet-time space has a purpose, and I need to stay focused.

So, for those few minutes before my day begins, I lie there thinking about the event. I let my mind roam through all of the details: from when the planning first began to where it is now. *Thank You, Jesus.* Deep things start to surface to my mind. Whatever big issue I have not had time to think about, to concentrate on, I allow myself to do so now. I walk through every scenario and play them out. The how to is revealed, the steps are laid out, and any dilemma comes together with a plan. I keep a pad and pen on my night table. I write down anything that now comes to mind. I draw, I scribble ideas, and I write down solutions.

---

[17] en.wikipedia.org/wiki/Noise.

Morning is only one time to find your quiet time. I have also found quiet time in the evenings, when I take a long stroll around the neighborhood. My objective is not to get in my daily thirty minutes of brisk walking; rather, its purpose is to allow mental time for my thoughts to have a conversation with God. I may walk a few steps and stop. I may find a bench and sit for a while. The occasional car that goes by or the barking of the dog in the distance are just white noise in the background.

In my walking quiet time, I usually find myself talking out loud. This does not disturb the occasional jogger, as with the rise of electronic ear devices nowadays, one can get away with talking to yourself. Typically, my evening-walk quiet time is to deal with any people issues. If I am having a dilemma working with someone or trying to figure out how to best reach someone who may not have returned my phone calls, texts, or e-mail messages, I use that time to strategize and seek God for His direction in dealing with others.

When can you find your quiet time? You may find, like me, it is just before I get out of bed or in the early evening. However, there are other times when the quiet can happen:

- driving in your car
- taking a bath or shower
- at the hair salon while under the dryer
- standing in long lines

Is there a particular length to the quiet time to make it successful? I don't think so. However, I have learned that what does *not* work is trying to find the quiet between commercials of your favorite TV show. I tried this one time and turned on the mute button and timed the commercial break, which was nearly seven minutes. The length of time to focus on one thing might have worked, except for the fact that I kept peeping at the screen to see if my show had returned!

Creating the quiet could be as short as five to ten minutes or as long as a few days. The longer quiet space is reflective of retreats, whether religious or secular. Many of us are familiar with retreats, and nowadays some groups call them "advances," rather than retreats. Even so, the premise is the same: dedicated time away to reflect, regroup, resurge, recommit, and reestablish, with the goal to leave that time having accomplished a predetermined goal. Whenever your quiet time may be, relish in it. For there you will enable your subconscious mind to speak so that you can hear it and hear God as well.

Keep the Devil out. The Enemy will try to make you believe the last thing you have time for is quiet time. If you are really struggling with a concept or idea, it may require a longer period of quiet, such as a retreat.

I recall a conference speaker giving the example of a group of automobile designers having difficulty coming up with a creative way to market a new car line at an upcoming national auto show. It was going to be tough competition. How in the world were they going to compete with a rival company that was going to have an ice rink built around its car, with models in bathing suits making figure eights around the cars? They packed up and went on a retreat.

After beating their heads for a few days, nothing. At some point, someone suggested going into town to see how people were "interacting" with their cars. As they stood on a corner in the middle of downtown, they realized something ... people were having conversations in their cars. Some were talking to their cars, and others were talking with people in their cars. Conversations were happening in the cars. Voila! Why not have cars talk back? They regrouped and feverishly came up with their marketing angle.

Months later at the auto show, they produced their new line. Ice-rink models were at one end of the exhibit hall, and their car line at the other. As people stood in line to see the car, a representative with a discreet microphone-hearing device would casually ask several questions such as, "What is your name?" "Are you looking for something special in a new car?" and so on. When the person got into the car, the car—you got it—would begin a conversation, which would go something like:

Individual settles in car.

Car: "Hello, (Name)."

Person [surprised, laughing]:   "What? Okay. Hello."

Car: "I am the type of car you are looking for in a new vehicle. This car gets thirty-five miles per gallon on the highway and twenty-five in the city. That would be very cost-effective for you with your long commute to work."

Person [more chuckling]:   "Yep, that sure would be."

Car: "Did Tom, our representative you met in line, tell you that *New Car Report* has our car listed as a five-star crash rating this year?"

Person: "No, I don't think Tom mentioned that. That's pretty good."

Car: "Family safety is important to us. Hi, Emily. Hi, Alex." (A little girl and teenage boy are sitting in the backseat.) "Hi," say Emily and Alex.

Car continues: "The car has great resale value and is rated highest among its peers. It would still be in great condition when Alex gets to drive it in five years. What do you think, Alex—do you like the car?"

[Teenager Alex's eyes light up just at the thought.] "Yeah. Dad, c'mon!"

Person: "Not sure about all that. But I do like the idea of good resale value."

Car: "Our other features include: dual seat heating, installed GPS at no extra charge to customer, and (continues with top features of the car)."

Person: "Well, that all sounds pretty impressive."

Car: "Thank you. I do think I'm pretty impressive. Is there anything I can answer while we're having this little chat?"

Person: "Not at this time. Thanks for the conversation!"

Car: "The pleasure is all mine, (Name). Kelly will meet you as you exit to give you more information about me. I hope to become a part of your family next year."

Person: "Yeah, thanks." (Chuckles as family gets out of car.)

Alex: "That was cool."

Emily: "That was fun. Bye, Car."

Car: "Bye, Emily."

The speaker stated that most conversations lasted between two to five minutes. Certainly, the longer a potential customer was in the car, the better chance of the customer thinking about the car when it came to market. The "talking car" became the hit of the auto show that year. And it all started with a group of designers finding quiet time in a most unusual spot—the middle of a busy intersection in a local city downtown. The quiet did not work in the cabin in the woods; rather, they had to be somewhere where they were able to focus their attention on one thing—people and cars.

Develop a Portfolio of Ideas

Other ideas to get your ideas flowing!

1. Create a portfolio:
    Keep an electronic or paper folder with event ideas, decorations, or thoughts about events that you have seen or that have come to your mind. I have often had to refer to my "idea" file when my mind draws a blank.

2. Talk with others:
    Call a friend or ask a colleague for ideas. Having someone with a fresh eye look at what you have done so far may help to generate possibilities, particularly when you get in a dry spell.

Scriptures

"Evening, and morning, and at noon, will I pray and cry aloud: and he shall hear my voice" (Ps. 55:17).

"Cast thy burden upon the Lord, and he shall sustain thee: he shall never suffer the righteous to be moved" (Ps. 55:22).

"The fear of the Lord is to hate evil: pride, and arrogancy, and the evil way and the forward mouth, do I hate" (Prov. 8:13).

PART 7

FINAL WORDS

"The grace of our Lord Jesus Christ be with you all. Amen."
—Revelation 22:21

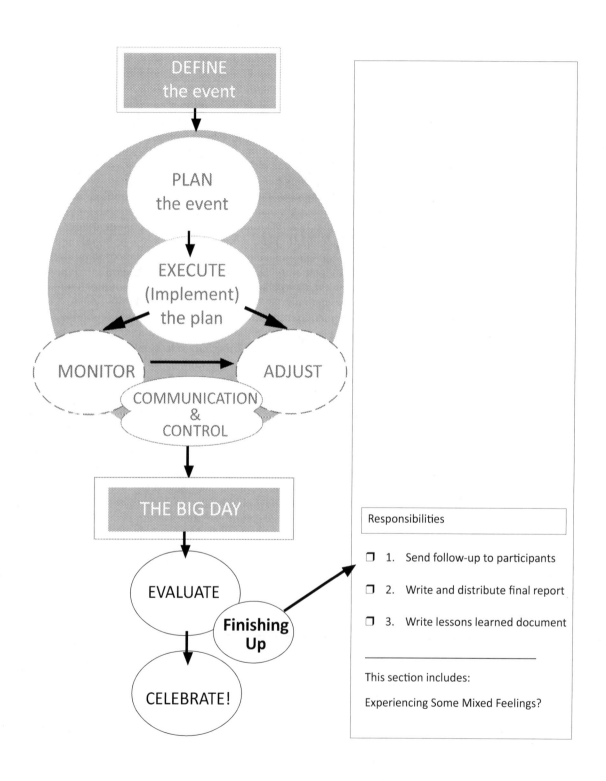

DEFINE
the event

PLAN
the event

EXECUTE
(Implement)
the plan

MONITOR → ADJUST

COMMUNICATION
&
CONTROL

THE BIG DAY

EVALUATE

Finishing Up

CELEBRATE!

Responsibilities

☐ 1. Send follow-up to participants

☐ 2. Write and distribute final report

☐ 3. Write lessons learned document

This section includes:

Experiencing Some Mixed Feelings?

CHAPTER 18

THE IMPORTANCE OF FOLLOW-UP

"A new commandment I give unto you, That ye love one another; as
I have loved you, that ye also love one another. By this shall all men
know that ye are my disciples, if ye have love one to another."
—John 13:34-35

Don't Leave 'Em Hanging

Every event should have some kind of follow-up with the participants to see if the event met their expectations. How will you know if you do not ask? People tend to gripe to others rather than the organizers, which does not help those planning the event.

One way to follow up is with an evaluation card or electronic evaluation. In addition to asking the standard questions such as what they did or did not like, ask if they had a particularly bad experience. If so, ask them to please allow you to make it up to them by sending them a gift card to a local restaurant.

Other ways to contact people after the event:

1. Follow up with a call or e-mail message.
2. Send a personal thank-you and include a brochure/pamphlet about the church.
3. Invite them out to the next event or to a smaller event with fewer members from the larger event.

Experiencing Some Mixed Feelings?

After the event, especially one that has taken six months or more to complete, you may not be feeling the exhilaration you thought you would. A common term used to describe this experience is *postpartum blues*.

Think about it. You have spent months devoting your time and energy to a specific event. Once it is successfully achieved, you may feel lost, directionless, and sad. No one is coming to you for direction, there are no more fires to put out, and there is no more thrill of seeing a major milestone come to pass.

Your symptoms may indeed be real. But do not be discouraged—another event is on the way! Remember:

- All events come to an end. Period.
- Thank those who helped plan the event.
- Write a final report or lessons-learned document, which will help you or others to learn from your successes and mistakes.
- And don't forget to celebrate!

TOOLS FOR SUCCESS

SAMPLE SPEAKER LETTERS

Sample Speaker Invitation Letter

Sample Speaker Follow-Up Letter

Date

Name
Church
Address
City, State, Zip

Dear (Name):

Greetings in the precious name of Jesus. The (church or organization) is eager to invite you to be the keynote speaker for our (event) on (day, date, year). The event will be held at (location, address, and pastor). Evening service begins at 6:30 p.m.

To tell you a little about our women's ministry, this year we celebrate our third annual conference. The conference was developed to create more opportunities for the sisters of our church to fellowship with one another and develop a better understanding of the Word of God and how it applies to their everyday lives. This event has become the largest event at the church, and we typically have approximately one hundred women in attendance.

We are prepared to offer you an honorarium of $_____ and will cover your hotel and airfare (or reimbursement for mileage at the government rate of .55 cents per mile). Should you accept this invitation, please contact me at (phone number and e-mail address) and let me know: your travel preferences, whether you want to fly in or drive, and your preference for hotel room (king or double bed). Also, please send a high-resolution photo and short bio that we can use in our marketing efforts. More information will be sent to you later with additional details.

We pray that you will be available to be our keynote speaker. and we look forward to hearing from you. Please respond to (e-mail address) or (phone number) by (date).

In Christ's service,

(Name)
(Title)
cc: (Pastor's or President's name)

Date

Name
Church
Address
City, State, Zip

Dear (Name):

Grace and peace. On behalf of our president (name) and the (church or organization), we write to confirm that you will be our evening speaker for the (event). The (event) will be held on (day, date, year) at (location).

Our theme for the conference is: (title). However, our general motto for the women's auxiliary is "I am victorious!" We will be praying for you in the months and days to come and trust that the Lord will give you the words to say to us that evening.

If you have any questions or concerns, please feel free to contact me by phone at (phone number) or e-mail at (address).

In Christ's service,

(Name)
(Title)

cc: (Pastor's or President's name)

Sample Completed Planning Time Line

Women's Conference
(Create a top sheet that lists main items)

Event: <u>Women's Conference</u>

Location: <u>Life Is Meaningful Community Church</u>

Date: <u>August 14, 2010</u>

Caterer: <u>Dan's Perfected Meals</u>

Printer: <u>OnTime Printers</u>

Florist: <u>Sally's Flowerland</u>

Planning begins: <u>January 2010</u>

Budget: <u>$4,500</u>

Last Update: 1.12.10/**3.11.10/5.5.10/5.19.10**
Final: **10/20/10**

Women's Conference
Planning Time Line
Conference Date: August 14, 2010
Sponsored by: Life is Meaningful Community Church
Theme: "Taking It All in Balance"

Purpose of Conference	Plan a relaxing and exciting one day conference for approximately seventy-five women on issues such as balancing work, life, and family.	
Project Lead and Core Planning Team	Katie Elam (KE), Mark Irish (MI), Kim Stanford (KS), Paula Thompson (PT), Darlene Randolf-Jackson (DRJ), Robin Samson (RS), Marilyn Weber (MW) and Denise Hanson (DH)	
Email Group Name	WomensConference2010@yahoo.com	
Event Manager	Lynne Shivers (LS)	
Reoccurring Theme/s	• Fellowship • Socializing • Prayers	
Targeted Audience	Women at LIMC and surrounding community (approx. 285)	
Expected Attendance	75-100 during day and excess of 200 for evening services	
Budget	$4,500	
Registration Fee	$55.00 per person	
Yearly Deliverables	• Schedule conference for mid-May	Completed 6/10/09
	• Select facility and secure all rooms needed	Completed 6/10/09
	• Select core planning team	Completed
	• Select meeting dates and times convenient for planning committee members	Completed 11/17/09
	• Assess needs and interest of audience	
	• Confirm theme is of interest and important to intended audience	Completed 2/10
	• Select keynote speaker	Completed 12/17/09
	• Select workshops and massages	Completed 2/25/10
	• Create reward system at conference (certificate in each participants folder)	Completed 5/18/10
	• Complete design of conference logo	Completed 3/5/10
	• Develop promotional communication materials	Completed
	• Conduct conference	Completed 5/26/10
	• Evaluate and debrief conference	Completed 6/17/10
	• Schedule next year's conference date	Completed. Next year's conference date: 8/13/11
Conference Date/Time	Sat., August 14, 2010; 8:00 am - 12:00 noon	
Location	Life is Meaning Community Church, 222 Your Town, USA 23451	
Keynote Speaker	Pastor Pam Sutherland, *Crossroads Church, Other Town, USA 23456*	
Theme	Taking It All in Balance	
Schedule	*Saturday, August 14, 2010* 7:00-8:00AM – Prayer 8:00-8:30AM – Continental Breakfast and Registration 8:30-4:00PM – Registration	

		8:45-9:45AM – Opening Remarks and Address
		10:00-11:00AM – Seminar 1
		11:10AM-12:10PM – Seminar 2
		12:10-1:00PM – Lunch
		1:00-2:00PM – Panel Discussion
		2:10-3:10PM – Seminar 3
		3:10-3:30PM – Fellowship in Grand Hall
		3:30-4:30PM- Closing program and Remarks
Breakout Sessions (workshops)		• The Me in Me Got in the Way of Us Again (f)
		• Getting Past the Mask to See You! (s)
		• How to Pray for Others and Not Get In Their Business (p)

TASK LISTING

#	TASK	Assigned to	Begin Date	End Date	%Complt	Notes
JANUARY						
1	Select date for next year's conference	LS	1/10/10	1/10/10	100%	
2	Ensure date is on pastor's calendar; send hold-the-date to LIMCC administration	LS	1/10/10	1/10/10	100%	
3	Discuss with pastor/leader the budgeted amount for this year	DRJ	1/10/10	1/10/10	100%	
4	Select committee members	ALL	1/10/10	1/10/20	100%	
FEBRUARY						
5	First meeting with committee members: initial discussion on goals, theme, workshop topics, and speakers	All	2/16/10	2/16/10	100%	
6	Develop detailed budget	LS	2/17/10	2/17/10	100%	
7	Meet with committee; continue discussion on items in #2. Review revised timeline and budget. Discuss key issues conference must address, keynote speaker, workshops	All	2/17/10	2/17/10	100%	Christian Humorist to speak on transitions; "Humor Lady"
8	Develop catchy theme title (Balancing It All)	All	2/17/10	2/17/10	100%	
9	Return signed contract	LS	2/17/10	2/17/10	100%	
10	Reserve Board Room for Registration Folder Stuffing Day	LS	2/17/10	2/18/010	100%	
11	Get event account for billing	RS			100%	
12	Contact speaker: Pastor Pam Sutherland	LS	2/17/10	2/21/10	100%	Pastor Sutherland agreed
13						
MARCH						
14	Meet with committee: finalize keynote speaker, determine workshop titles and potential speakers, assign who will make initial contact to seminar speakers	All	3/14/10	3/14/10	100%	
15	Draft Speaker AV confirmation letter and AV Needs form	LS	Moved to April	Moved to April	100%	
16	Initial contact to workshop speakers	KE	3/10/10	3/10/10	100%	
17	Inform Sis. Lynne of speakers' consent to speak; send speaker contact information (e-mail address, etc) to her	All	3/11/10	3/12/10	100%	
18	Initial inquiry to main speaker if she consents to speak, send contact information to Sis. Lynne	LS	3/17/10	3/17/10	100%	Done as Lynne was the contact with the

						speaker
19	Design conference logo to work with Sis. Kim	KE/LS	3/11/10	3/5/10	100%	
20	Design date saver present to committee	LS	3/11/10	3/11/10	100%	
21						
22						
APRIL						
23	Review evaluation methods	Mgrs/LS	--	4/25/10	100%	
24	Develop first draft of program as it will flow: times for main speaker and workshops, review options for promoting event (web, e-mail, flier, date saver, etc), discuss purpose/benefits of attending	All	4/11/10	4/25/10	100%	
25	Send confirmation letter to keynote speaker	LS	4/11/10	4/18/10	100%	
26	Send confirmation letter to seminar speakers	LS	4/11/10	4/11/10	100%	
27	Arrange lodging for main speaker, if needed	LS	n/a	n/a	n/a	
28	Contact caterer for continental breakfast and snacks	LS	4/11/10	4/11/10	100%	Caterer will bring samples to next mtg (4/25?)
29	Finish date saver design, include e-RSVP, get approval from committee	LS	4/11/10	4/18/10	100%	
30						
31						
32						
33						
34						
35						
MAY						
36	Meet with committee	All	5/11/10	5/11/10	100%	
37	Send out communication w/Promo Piece	DRJ/RS	5/31/10	5/31/10	100%	
38	Develop evaluation questions to determine whether goals of conference were met	ALL	5/25/10		100%	
39	Develop evaluation instrument in draft form based on questions above	RS	5/25/10	7/1/10	100%	
40	Prepare sample registration form	LS	5/18/10	5/25/10	100%	To be ready by April 2
41	Determine any others to invite to conference	ALL	5/25/10	5/25/10	100%	At the 5/3 Mtg
42	Serve as liaison to Sis. Lynne for program	KE	ongoing	ongoing	100%	
43	Obtain/Create list of area restaurants	PT	5/25/10	6/1/10	100%	
44	Lunch options for staff/volunteers onsite	ALL	5/25/10	6/8/10	100%	
45	Discuss how conference opening will flow: who's on program, introductions, etc	ALL	4/11/10	5/8-22/10	100%	
46	Prepare conference brochure mailing to go out first of April	LS	4/11/10	4/31/10	100%	
47	Select volunteers for: Facilitating each workshop (based on # of seminars)	LS	4/25/10	4/25/10	100%	

#	Task	Who	Start	End	%	Notes
48	Determine from committee who will introduce main speaker, discuss any pending issues?	All	4/25/10	5/8/10	100%	
49						

JUNE						
50	Identify on-site registration needs, how long to leave registration open	RS/LS	6/10/10	6/14/10	95%	Placed in script to discuss at 5/20 mtg
51	Arrange transportation/pick-up for main speaker	LS	n/a	n/a	n/a	None needed, speaker is on campus
52	Request photographer	RS	6/12/10	6/12/10	100%	John Smith Photography
53	Determine payment process with budget administrator	LS	6/10/10	6/10/10	85%	Received all payment forms
54	Determine if music will be played as participants enter dining room	LS	6/22/10	6/20/10	100%	
55	Determine weekly meetings schedule/location	ALL	6/22/10	6/22/10	100%	To discuss at 7/6 mtg
56	Determine registration supplies needed (programs, pens, paper pads, tissue, water bottle, etc)	RS	6/22/10	7/17/20	100%	
57	Contact seminar speakers (confirm date, time, AV needs). Need their ppt slides or flash drive by (XXX) to load on laptops.	LS	6/11/10	6/15/10	100%	

JULY-AUGUST						
58	Prepare room-needs request form and send to LIMCC Office two weeks before conference	LS	7/11/10	7/11/10	100%	Due to Kris, done by LS.
59	Assign workshop rooms based on registration counts	LS	7/22/10	8/12/10	100%	
60	Send itinerary to main speaker	LS	7/19/10	7/19/10	100%	
61	Coordinate printing of final program	LS	7/5/10	7/6/10	100%	Draft presented at mtg by DRJ
62	Prepare moderator instructions for volunteers who are assigned to introduce speakers	LS	7/5/10	7/5/10	100%	DRJ to present at next mtg
63	Get parking signs for speakers	RS	7/10/10	7/21/10	100%	
64	Create direction and rooms signage	LS	7/17/10	7/21/10	100%	
65	Prepare instructions if needed	LS	n/a	n/a	n/a	
66	Review list of participants, give counts to caterer and graphic designer	LS	7/5/10	7/21/10	100%	At close = 103 registered
67	Prepare important instructions for staff/volunteers	ALL	7/6/10	7/20/10	100%	Present at next mtg
68	Design name badges (keynote & workshop speakers, volunteers, VIPs)	RS	7/6/10	7/19/10	100%	
69	Develop script of entire day	LS	7/10/10	7/20/10	100%	
70	Order supplies (folders, name tags, etc)	RS	7/3/10	7/21/10	100%	
71	Remind speakers to forward ppt slides by (XX)	LS	7/10/10	7/18/10	n/a	Bringing flash drive per AV request form
72	Determine if music will be played as participants enter main room	LS	7/22/10	7/22/10	100%	No music
73	Remind speakers to bring ppt on flash drive	LS	8/2/10	8/12/10	n/a	See #71
73a	Select day for Registration Bag stuffing	RS	8/6/10	8/18/10	100%	

73b						
ONE WEEK BEFORE EVENT						
74	Load laptops with ppt slides from seminar speakers	n/a	n/a	n/a	100%	
75	Select music to be played as participants enter main room	n/a	n/a	n/a	100%	
76						
77						
78						
WEEK OF EVENT						
79	Hold Registration folder stuffing day	RS	8/6/10	8/18	100%	
80	Reminder sent to participants	LS	8/24/10	8/24/10	100%	
81	Review payment forms for speakers	LS	8/20/10	8/24/10		
82						
83						
84						
DAY OF EVENT						
85	Members arrival times to assist with set up of tables in Assembly Hall and Registration area	LS/RS	8/14/10	8/14/10	100%	Arrive at 6:30am Others at 7am
86	Inspect rooms: AV needs, etc	LS	8/14/10	8/14/10	100%	
87	Monitor transportation arrangements	LS	8/14/10	8/14/10	100%	
88	Send electronic questionnaire to participants	RS	8/14/10	8/14/10	100%	
89						
90						
POST EVENT						
91	Schedule post meeting with planning committee	RS	8/17/10	8/17/10	100%	
92	Review evaluation results with planning committee	RS	8/24/10	8/16/10	100%	
93	Review evaluation results with pastor/program director	Lead Team	9/10/10	9/10/10	100%	
94	Send thank-you letters to speakers with evaluation results	LS	9/15/10	9/16/10	100%	
95	Prepare and final reports and distribute	LS/RS	10/12/10	10/14/10	100%	
96	Review "lessons learned" and file in binder or folder for next year	LS	10/17/10	10/17/10		Discuss at debrief mtg
97	Reserve next year's date for conference	LS	--	--	100%	Next year: 8/13/11
98						
99						
100						

SAMPLE WOMEN'S CONFERENCE BUDGET

Women's Conference Budget

Projected Budget: $4,500.00
Final Budget: $4,327.70
Projected Registration/Income $5,500.00
Actual Registration: $4,675.00
Over/(Under) - $347.30 Savings!

	Projected Expenses	Actual	Item
Speaker(s) Travel/Hotel/Honoria			
1.	$500.00	$500.00	Speaker: Pastor Pam Sutherland
2.	$1,000.00	$750.00	Workshop Speakers (3 x $250 ea)
3.	$500.00	$535.62	Air travel (Keynote speaker)
4.	$258.00	$233.86	JW Marriott (keynote spkr 2 nights)
	$2,258.00	**$2,019.48**	**Speakers Total**
Venue			
5.	$0.00	$0.00	LIMCC
6.	$150.00	$150.00	Custodial services Saturday
	$150.00	**$150.00**	**Venue Total**
Food and Beverage			
7.	$175.00	$149.47	Panera Breakfast (continental deluxe)
8.	$900.00	$1,020.00	Dan's Perfected Meals ($12 x 85 pp)
9.	$125.00	$150.00	Sally's Flowerland (buffet centerpiece)
	$1,075.00	**$1,319.47**	**F&B Total**
Publicity and Photography			
10.	$350.00	$350.00	Graphic Designer - Sis. Suellen Winters
11.	$125.00	$0.00	Photographer (Bro. Phillip Peabody)
	$475.00	**$350.00**	**P&A Total**
Registration			
12.	$500.00	$488.75	OnTime Printers - Print program books
13.	$42.00	$0.00	Supplies (pens, pads, facial tissue and waterbottles donated by LIMCC Nurses)
14.	$0.00	$0.00	Participants' Certificates of Appreciation
	$542.00	**$488.75**	**Registration Total**
	$4,500.00	**$4,327.70**	**TOTAL**

BUFFET-TABLE PHOTO COMPARISON

This T-setup buffet table is very bland. Although the caterer tried to use floral pink and white overlays to create interest, it still lacks visual appeal.

Compared to another T-setup in the same room, this buffet has more visual interest because the caterer used the food to create color and frozen glass blocks to elevate trays to entertain the eye. I tend to use small boxes and cover them with swatches of fabric to elevate the food and dessert trays (you can also use color linen napkins).

Let's Talk Details

Here are a few questions to think about when planning your event:

1. How will people know we care about them?
2. What shall we do if a critical resource leaves during the planning stages or a volunteer does not show up on the day of the event?
3. What if it rains?
4. What if the air-conditioner goes out or the heat goes on the blink?
5. What if people are not responding to our invitations—what do we do?
6. When should we cancel the event? How will we let people know?
7. What if the programs do not arrive on time?
8. What kind of fund-raising can we do to keep registration costs down for the participants?
9. What can we do differently this year to make the event more interesting than last year's?
10. Is there a group we're missing that could attend but are not? How can we remove real or perceived obstacles?

MAKE YOUR PASSION YOUR PROFESSION

Has the event bug bitten you? Do you want to learn more about the event-planning industry? Possibly you are interested in starting your own event-planning business? Here are some ideas that can get you started in the event industry.

1. Do your homework and develop contacts with national and location event-planning associations. Contact them via e-mail or phone and request information about their educational and networking programs and resources.
2. Join a professional organization in your area. Many national event-planning organizations have state chapters that have regular meetings and events. This is a great way to get yourself acclimated to the organization and meet with other event planners in your local area.
3. Set goals that includes becoming increasingly involved in the local chapter (such as serving on committees and volunteering at events).
4. Stay updated on new trends and technology in the event industry.
5. Attend local events to get ideas you can draw from.

In summary, as with any career, it is going to take hard work. James 1:4 tell us, "Let patience have her perfect work..." Be deliberate and diligent. Ask God for direction and guidance along the way. Allow any perceived failure to be a learning experience. Every misfortune, mistake, fiasco and disappointment can be turned into a learning experience that will help you later. You *can* be successful in this business. May the peace of God be with you!

ABOUT THE AUTHOR

Lynne Shivers is an author, speaker, licensed minister, and project and event manager. She has more than thirty years' experience in planning events for academic institutions and religious organizations. She teaches event-planning workshops the University of Michigan, Michigan State University, and event-planner organizations. Lynne has served as president of the University of Michigan University Event Planners organization and is currently a member of the Religious Conference Management Association and All Things Artistic Ministries, Inc. Christian writers. She is a minister and Sunday School teacher at Greater Grace Temple, Taylor, Michigan, under the pastorate of Bishop Gary Harper. Evangelist Shivers was also president of the Missionary and Christian Women's Auxiliary of the Northern District Council for the Pentecostal Assemblies of the World, Inc. She holds a bachelor's degree in psychology from Bowie State University and a master's degree in educational psychology from the University of Michigan. Lynne is married to Elder Jonathan Shivers Jr. They live in Ypsilanti, Michigan.

Contact Lynne at:

lynneshivers@yahoo.com
lynneshivers.com

WORKS CITED

Note: As a reminder, long before I started writing my book, I had been collecting information and attending many event-planning workshops and conferences. At times I neglected to record the source of materials. Although I have been able to track down many of the authors, there are some I could not find.

Anderson, E. S. "Your Church's Facebook Page." Posted June 15, 2011. *http://sowhatfaith.com/2011/06/15/your-churchs-facebook-page/*.

Biblos, B. B. *Gills Exposition of the Entire Bible*. Biblehub: http:bible.cc/isaiah/12-5.htm.

Fortini-Campbell, Lisa. *Hitting the Sweet Spot*. Chicago: The Copy Workshop, a division of Bruce Bendinger Creative Communications, Inc., 2001, pages 24-28

The Free Dictionary by Farlex. http://www.freedictionary.com/excellent.

Freeman, J. M. *The New Manners Customs of the Bible*. North Brunswick, NJ: Bridge-Logos Publishers, 1998, page 294

Goldblatt, Joe, and Kathleen S. Nelson. *The International Dictionary of Event Management (The Wiley Event Management Series)*. New York: John Wiley & Sons, Inc., 2001, page 78

Houseal, Rich, and Dale Jones. *2010 U.S. Religion Census: Religious Congregations & Membership Study,* Nazarene Publishing House, Lenexa, KS, page 6

Lindner, E. W. *Yearbook of American and Canadian Churches*. New York: Abingdon Press, Nashville, 2010, page 8

McClelland, M. "How Do I Become A Better Fisherman?" *Walleye Central*: *http://www.walleyecentral.com/articles/?a=7*

Merriam-Webster Dictionary. www.merriam-webster.com/dictionary/perfect.

Miller, D. A. *Maverick Marketing ... on a shoestring budget!* Kansas City, MO: Board Report Publishing Co., Inc., 2004, page 5

Paton, J. "Chastisement and the Christian." *http://www.eternalsecurity.us/ chastisement_and_the_christian.htm.*

Robinson, R. D. *Bible Study: The Seven Feasts of Israel Leviticus 23:1–44. http:www. brandonweb.com/sermons/sermonpages/leviticus2.htm.*

Rutherford Silvers, Julie. *Package and Manage an Experience by Mastering the A's of Events.* International Special Events Society Conference.

Thompson, C. *Shocking Beliefs of the Unchurched.* Posted on the *Anchorage Daily News* website November 30, 2008: http://community.adn.com/ node/135135#ixzz1Ub240Uiz.

en.wikipedia.org/wiki/Noise.